A CEILING OF SKY

A CEILING OF SKY

Special Garden Rooms and the People Who Created Them

PAT ROSS

with photographs by the author

TIME
LIFE

Alexandria, Virginia

TIME LIFE BOOKS

Time-Life Books is a division of Time Life Inc.

TIME LIFE INC.
PRESIDENT AND CEO
Jim Nelson

TIME-LIFE TRADE PUBLISHING
VICE PRESIDENT AND PUBLISHER
Neil Levin
SENIOR DIRECTOR OF ACQUISITIONS AND EDITORIAL RESOURCES
Jennifer Pearce
DIRECTOR OF NEW PRODUCT DEVELOPMENT Carolyn Clark
DIRECTOR OF MARKETING Inger Forland
DIRECTOR OF NEW PRODUCT DEVELOPMENT Teresa Graham
DIRECTOR OF TRADE SALES Dana Hobson
DIRECTOR OF CUSTOM PUBLISHING John Lalor
DIRECTOR OF SPECIAL MARKETS Robert Lombardi
DIRECTOR OF DESIGN Kate L. McConnell

A CEILING OF SKY
DIRECTOR OF CREATIVE SERVICES Laura McNeill
SENIOR EDITOR Linda Bellamy
TECHNICAL SPECIALIST Monika Lynde
PRODUCTION MANAGER Carolyn Bounds
QUALITY ASSURANCE Jim King, Stacy L. Eddy

BOOK DESIGN BY HOWARD KLEIN
ILLUSTRATIONS BY PAT LALTRELLA

Pre-Press Services, Time-Life Imaging Center
Printed in Canada.
1 3 5 7 9 10 8 6 4 2

Time-Life is a trademark of Time Warner Inc., and affiliated companies.

Library of Congress Cataloging-in-Publication Data
Ross, Pat.
A ceiling of sky : special garden rooms and the people who create them /
by Pat Ross.
    p.   cm.
ISBN 0-7370-0611-0 (hc.)
    1. Landscape gardening. 2. Garden rooms. 3. Gardeners. I. Title.
SB473 .R64   2000
712.6--dc21   99-057162

Books produced by Time-Life Trade Publishing are available at a special
bulk discount for promotional and premium use. Custom adaptations can
also be created to meet your specific marketing goals. Call 1-800-323-5255.

ACKNOWLEDGMENTS
MANY PEOPLE TO THANK

I'd like to thank my many gardening and non-gardening friends and thoughtful acquaintances who saw me through this project. So thank you to Kenny Ball and Betsy Sheffield at Kenny Ball Antiques in Charlottesville, Virginia; Geoffrey and Joan Bell; Carolyn Bucha; Charlotte Frischkorn; Jose and Lisa Gaytan; Eileen Imber, with special thanks for letting me see her wonderful garden designs in Manhattan; Gillian Jolis; Jennifer Lee; Betsy and Chris Little; Lucy and Paul McKean; Linda Parker; Margie Rexrode and the staff at Morning Glories and Moonflowers in Monterey, Virginia; Gail Rock; Wendy Sarasohn; Anastasia Vournas; Barbara and John Wilkerson; Geri Williams; Lucy Williams; and Gigi Zimmer.

My continuing gratitude goes to everyone at Time-Life Books, including Linda Bellamy, Inger Forland, Kate Hartson, Neil Levin, Denise McGann, Jennifer Stowe, and Olga Vezeris. Thanks also to the invaluable outside support team: Owen Andrews, Marc Berenson, Barbara Clark, Leisa Crane, and Orietta Ramirez.

My enduring thanks to Howard Klein for the enormous care he's taken with my photography, giving the words and the images a most elegant presentation. Pat Laltrella did double duty, as featured gardener and as artist, creating the drawings that add considerable charm to the book.

The gardeners and garden experts who opened their gates and their files to me were numerous. They include Lemeau Arrott-Watt and Richard Duckett; Halstead Wells; Steve Beacham and Gary Eagan; Judi Boisson and her wonderful staff at Judi Boisson Home Collection in Southampton, New York; Margaret Burnett at Gardenmaker, whose thoughtfulness reached as far as my Virginia garden; Suzanne Coe for her garden designs; Phyllis Cothran and Arnie Stolberg; Christy and Dave Cottrell; Irene and Bill Douglass; Cynthia Dupps, who owns the shop Pump & Circumstances in Eureka Springs, Arkansas, and her husband, Kirk Dupps, as well as David Wiseman; Peter Ermacora and Evan Hughes; Holly and Jay Ertel; Margie Farinholt, owner of Robert Blair Antiques in Richmond, Virginia, who developed her garden in collaboration with Jim Farinholt of Precision Landscape in Richmond; Catherine Gevers and John X. Fernandez; The Hancock Shaker Museum, especially Lawrence Yerden and Sharon Koomler; Betty and George Kramer; Sue Ann and Ted Marolda and Lissette Benitez Moguel; Douglas and Billy Martin and their contractor, Steve Berg of Berg Construction in Richmond, Virginia; Charles Muise and Gene Heil; Anne Newman and Joe Bacal, who are thankful to Vance Stevens and Julie Cummins; Molly and John Seeligson; Karen Skelton and Richard Siegel, whose garden things from their pottery, PotLuck Studios in Accord, New York, make a show in any garden, and who are assisted by the very helpful Donna McConnell; Janet Thompson, Douglas Martin's partner at Paper Plus in Richmond, Virginia; Beth Tudor, with special thanks for having gardening parents, Mary Alice and Penn Tudor; Phyllis Warden; and Pattie and Mason Williams.

When, finally, it's time to thank my family, usually the book has run out of space, yet it would be impossible for me to run out of appreciation for their constant gifts of patience and love. Ken McGraw, a fine photographer in his own right, has accompanied me to many gardens. My daughter, Erica Ross, provided loving support. For constant support, there's no one equal to my mother, Anita Kienzle, my sister, Jeanne Kienzle, and my aunt, Jerri Fowler. Thanks also to Alix Lynch and Bryan McGraw for keeping an eye on our garden at Hayfields Farm.

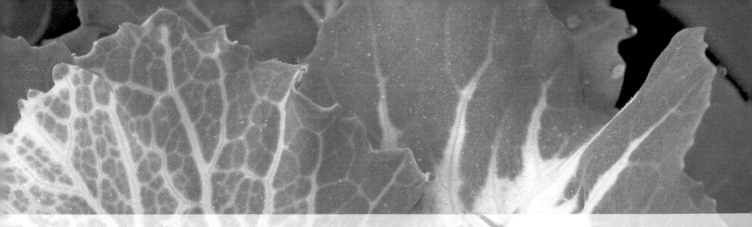

CONTENTS

INTRODUCTION
A Guest in Other Gardens 9

A VIEW WITH A ROOM
Planning for an Out-of-Doors Lifestyle 20

THE PERFECT FOUNDATION
A Sunken Walled Garden from the Past 34

CALIFORNIA MAGIC
A Garden for Entertaining 48

BEYOND POTLUCK
Creative Instincts for Entertaining Outdoors 60

A LIFE OF GARDENING
English Viewpoint, American Style 74

NATURE AT ARM'S LENGTH
A Screened Garden House 86

DESPERATELY SEEKING SOLITUDE
A Cottage Porch and a Garden Dilemma 98

THE GARDEN PATHS TAKEN
Green Links Among Family and Friends 106

BLOOMS AND COUNTERPOINT
Finding Roses and Paradise in a City Setting 122

FORM FOLLOWS FUNCTION
A Spontaneous One-Room Garden Plan 132

THE CHANGING FACE OF A GARDEN
Playing to Spectacular Borrowed Spaces 144

GARDEN SHELTER WITH A PAST
A Grape Arbor Centers a Lawn 156

DIVIDED BY THREE
Neighborly Hillside Gardens 168

STROLLING THE SKYLINE
A Terrace Turned Pocket Park 186

MANY ROOMS OF HER OWN
Creating Whimsical Spaces and Solitary Places 194

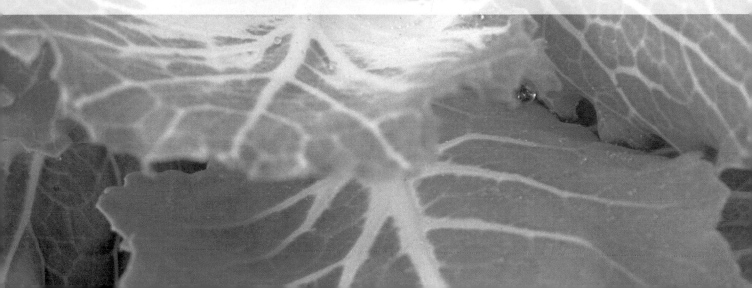

A GUEST IN OTHER GARDENS

OFTEN, I'VE BEEN a grateful guest in other people's gardens—reclining on a friend's comfortable lounge chair, a chilly drink in one hand and a good book on my lap; dining under the stars in fine style on someone else's terrace; having my morning coffee overlooking a lawn I don't have to mow. When I look through the lens of my camera, I'm in a unique position to record the most perfect moments in these gardens—when morning dew clings to every petal or the fading sunset makes a butter-yellow farewell. There's joy for me in finding beauty and balance in these borrowed gardens, and I've reaped my pleasures guiltlessly, without having to deadhead sweeps of lavender or pull a single weed. Yet all along, I've held fast to a secret longing to have a real garden to call home.

I got my chance when my partner, Ken McGraw, and I finally finished rebuilding—more like reinventing—an 1880 Victorian house on a farm in the western mountains of Virginia. The house sits on a windswept knoll in a spectacular and panoramic setting—three old trees shading the porch and nothing except a substantial hay barn to block the view. The main role of the fence is to keep the cows in, and any neigh-

FACING: One of a number of arches on Phyllis Warden's property in New York State—a garden I had the privilege of visiting during the course of this book—leads from one garden room to the next. There's a certain pleasurable anticipation in seeing only part of what's ahead and having to go through a doorway to find out.

RIGHT: Cynthia Dupps calls the waitress a flea market "fun find" for her daughter Holly's deck. Repainted bright red and given dark stocking seams with a thin brush, this full-figured conversation piece is an amusing take-off on Jeeves the butler, without his class.

PRECEDING PAGES: By sheer coincidence, my schedules for restoring and expanding an 1880 Virginia farmhouse with Ken McGraw at Hayfields Farm—seen here several years ago in its original haunted-house state—and creating this garden book ran parallel to each other. If, over the last century, anyone planted as much as a single bulb on the property, there was not a daffodil to show for it. With this clean slate and a natural backdrop that boggles the mind, I started my first garden.

ABOVE: During two and a half years of construction on the Hayfields house and then the garden, the front porch was the only uncluttered open-air place where Ken and I could sit, often on dilapidated old chairs. Before work on the house itself was completed, we installed a wooden porch swing, treating ourselves to a view of the stonemason's creative labors—a wall that pulls one part of the garden together.

RIGHT: Our backyard might have stretched for miles were it not for a brick terrace and stone wall that adjoin the new addition to our renovated farmhouse, shown here in a shot that was taken three years ago, during construction. Unfortunately, the wide brick stairway to heaven stopped us visually at the cattle fence, diminishing the magnificent view beyond. So that the fence wouldn't hit us in the face, we decided to move it back sixty feet or so, then create a wide-open garden room—perhaps a grove of pines and native bushes—somewhere on the hillside. At least, that was the plan.

boring property lines are down the road a piece. If anyone before me had ever planted a flower on the property, it was so long ago that even Mother Nature has forgotten its name.

My first real garden lies bordered by the gentle slope of Bullpasture Mountain, a view of the Bullpasture River, and a winding road along the Bullpasture Valley. All this adds up to quite a lot of bull and an overwhelming canvas on which to paint a lawn chair.

Recently, I ran into a friend I hadn't seen for years, someone who knew me before I embarked on phase two of what Ken likes to call our twenty-year garden plan—certainly long before I'd begun work on *A Ceiling of Sky*. I was struggling with a shopping bag filled with new garden books, their glossy jacket copy assuring me that I, too, could accomplish remarkable things and even master intimidating Latin botanical names. My friend laughed when she spotted all those books, remembering that I'm wildly allergic to poison ivy and can't pinch off a geranium leaf without getting a rash. I will admit to gardening for many years with safe potted plants in my New York City apartment—

mostly succulents, which seem to thrive on neglect—and to having an inborn eagerness for things to pop up overnight. Then I got hooked on container gardening when I owned a house near the beach. The property was the size of a postage stamp, but we had a spacious deck and I planted marvelous annuals—always a new color scheme each year—which soon spilled over the sides of the many boxes and pots that contained them. I smiled slyly and told my friend that I've learned many things about gardening over the years, not the least of which are patience and being a good observer.

When I started to work on *A Ceiling of*

ABOVE: During our first summer in residence, our main gathering place and the surrounding area showed noticeable progress. Adopting a Fred and Wilma Flintstone theme throughout the property, we used arrangements of enormous local rocks to break up the sweeping expanses and create intimate garden rooms. Once the cattle fence is moved back, we'll grade the old pasture and plant grass for croquet and badminton. Even though we transplanted some flowers from another garden, my yearned-for perennial beds have taken a back seat to the essential shape and structure of the new garden. But now that I've discovered magnificent daylilies with names like El Desperado and Country Melody, I intend to go wild come spring.

Sky, I envisioned this book as a companion of sorts to my previous gardening book, *Decorating Your Garden*. It surprised me by becoming so much more—especially for me, because I was just starting to plan my own garden. So when I interviewed the garden owners for this book, instead of simply recording how they had used their outdoor spaces, I began to look at their gardens as lessons for my own—their solutions for the problems that confronted them had much to teach me about planning my own space.

I learned that if you plant flowers, you must have a plan for how people are going to spend their time enjoying them. This doesn't happen overnight, unless you call in a team of experts and hand over the key to the garden gate. I learned that before you fall in love with a magnificent Victorian cast-iron dining set, you really ought to have a special place in mind for it. (However, if you can't help yourself, you'll store it in the shed until you find a place.)

Sometimes I learned the obvious: if you throw big parties, then you need lots of elbow room, whereas the opportunities are endless for more intimate gatherings. And if you prefer being alone with your thoughts,

ABOVE: Janet Thompson, a Virginia gardener, placed a rustic garden bench in the middle of breathtaking spring perennials as a whimsical way to say "welcome."

then a bench under a sheltering tree may be your idea of paradise. I learned the more subtle lessons as well, such as the fact that the best plans are the ones that express your individual personality.

At our farm in Virginia, the mornings are misty, the summer evenings are cool, and there's not a mosquito for several counties, making Hayfields Farm the perfect place to be outdoors. It's rare indeed to be blessed with such majestic mountain scenery, but when I searched for a cozy plan for our gathering spaces at the farm, the garden kept getting lost in the view. So Ken and I made a list of all the ways we wanted to use our outdoor spaces. Swinging on the front porch was at the top of our list, so we installed an old-fashioned wooden slatted swing and two rockers long before the interior was finished. Often, in the evenings, before the renovation was completed, we'd sneak onto the property like trespassers to sit on that swing and watch the sun drop behind Mount Carlyle. Once, we dragged along a bottle of wine and fine crystal glasses and set them on a silver tray. Then the plumber drove up, unannounced, and gave us the strangest look. A garden room like the ones in my book—the first of many garden rooms that we'd develop on the property—had begun to take shape.

Because I write books about home design as well as garden design, I look at outdoor

ABOVE: I had arrived at the home of the California gardener featured in this book only moments before spotting an arrangement of roses so magnificent that they became my first shot.

spaces in much the same way in which I look at the rooms of a house. I look for a garden's unique arrangement—the patterns of the plantings as well as the artful touches that extend personal living styles out-of-doors. *A Ceiling of Sky* is filled with seventeen unique gardens—each becoming an engaging short story about real-life gardeners who have created special places to enjoy life out-of-doors. There's no blueprint here for a gazebo or pattern for a stone terrace; no step-by-step plan. The challenges and victories found in the seventeen gardens carry the message I really want to convey.

Challenged by constricted spaces, densely tangled overgrowth, slopes better suited to mountain trails, or rubble-filled yards that look like demolition sites, most of the garden owners in *A Ceiling of Sky* began with properties that bore no resemblance to the "after" images on these pages. One or two gardeners were slightly more fortunate, for their inherited spaces were merely characterless or run-down: a boring lawn that rolled on indefinitely; unsightly outbuildings and a well cover blocking the view; a parking area with the dimensions and charm of a tennis

From the start, all of the gardeners profiled in this book knew they wanted their gardens to feel like home.

I studied these gardens through the lens of my camera. Frame by frame, I'd break up the larger spaces into manageable vignettes to see how these spaces worked independently, then came together, much like the rooms of a house. Indeed, many of the garden rooms were tangible structures: rustic garden dwellings that reminded me of my old 4-H camp; an open garden room with a cathedral-style ceiling painted blue like the sky; a rose arbor just big enough to inspire dinner for two; thoughtfully designed pergolas to center, to shade, to enfold; the kinds of comfortable porches our grandparents favored; arbor structures that give new meaning to dining alfresco. Other garden rooms were virtual; their spaces were defined by furniture that suited them and that became extensions of the house. The secret spaces were well worth the search made by a garden visitor looking for solitude.

Finally, with our home in Virginia completed and this book project well along, I began to plan for my own garden. I wanted our outdoor garden rooms to be in keeping with the style of our rebuilt Victorian farmhouse, which had, admittedly, assumed a few delusions of grandeur along the way.

As our plan progressed, bluestone pathways became the outdoor hallways; a struggling lawn became a somewhat threadbare carpet; the sky became the endless ceiling. I

court. All had acquired these properties for more redeeming features: a fabulous view, fine old shade trees, a quiet street, a patch of earth in a crowded city. All saw their property's potential, even if their dreams were slow to materialize. The gardeners are all linked by a desire to spend long hours in their gardens—beyond the planting, the weeding, and the admiring. Most of the gardeners in this book have spent years tending the same garden. The remaining garden owners are intrepid newcomers in their hard-won spaces.

ABOVE: It was other people's gardens that gave me ideas for my own, such as creating a charming gathering space only steps from the doorway long before the greater garden has had time to catch up. This arrangement shows that pieces of furniture can be enclosed by potted evergreens to create, literally, a living room.

envisioned entertaining on the terrace and planned that space with friends and family in mind. Ken and I joked that we'd toss sweet feed over the nearby fence to lure the cows to become our decorative accessories because black-and-white is always in vogue. When the view from a small screened porch off the kitchen needed a more intimate garden tableau, I planted an herb garden just outside the door and placed my favorite tall echinacea close to the screens for its color and charm.

Then I remembered something I'd jotted down from an antiquarian gardening book in my growing collection: "How necessary it is that garden furniture be convenient and appropriate; that proper resting places be provided to ensure the fullest enjoyment of the garden by ourselves and our friends." That timeless advice inspired me to envision garden rooms beyond the confines of our home garden. For fishing or just contemplating, even a pond got a unique stool made from a tractor seat. I'll admit that I tend to get carried away, but, after all, we have the space to dream. So if that is what's going on in my garden, I can blame it on being a guest in other gardens.

A View with a Room
Planning for an Out-of-Doors Lifestyle

WHEN DOUGLAS MARTIN moved to the 1927 cottage-style stone house designed and built by the noted architect Ernest Flagg, a proper garden—or, rather, the lack of one for half a century—was very much on her mind. Two hot-pink azalea bushes enjoyed their brilliant moment every spring, but otherwise there was not a single flower. Happily, if anyone could bring the soul of a gardener to the property, it was Douglas, a delicate woman named for a

PRECEDING PAGE: An Atlanta, Georgia, decorative painter named Jane Keltner used a bold stripe motif for the dining table, adding an occasional floral design for interest. A set of vintage French cafe chairs have been painted to coordinate.

ABOVE: Douglas Martin began decorating with unusual birdhouses long before collecting them became popular. For anyone sitting in the garden room, these many fascinating focal points draw attention to full plantings and colorful blooms.

FACING, TOP: The backyard's checkered history of structures has included a trellis covered with wisteria that never bloomed, an enclosed sunroom that opened onto a spacious slate terrace that baked in the sun, and an awning that leaked. Finally, Douglas and Billy Martin came up with a plan for the perfect sheltered structure out-of-doors—an open garden room with a classical half-pitch roof, unblocked by screens or partitions and supported by six classical Tuscan columns made of fiberglass.

FACING, BOTTOM: The bench's clean lines hint of a Gothic accent, but its true origins remain a mystery. Found in good condition, it required only a coat of green paint and a shady spot by the fence to fit right in.

grandfather who, rather fittingly, grew roses and arranged flowers.

Douglas is the sort of avid gardener who can wax eloquent about discovering a blue pea vine or training a rose called Paul's Himalayan musk to climb the pine trees out front. For many years, she's been involved in a significant way in a local Virginia garden club that's a member of the Garden Club of America. So, from the start, she had a vision of an American version of an English cottage garden to suit the house.

Newly married in 1981, she and her husband, Billy Martin, began making yearly trips to England, where they toured the splendid gardens, gathering ideas. Back home, Douglas used garden hoses to lay out the boundaries of major perennial beds, shaping the borders so they would face the back of the house. Soon the garden emerged as a gathering place where the Martins found themselves spending more and more time.

The backyard has had a checkered history of sheltering structures. First, there was a trellis with wisteria, but wisteria can be tricky and theirs never bloomed. Then a small enclosed sunroom was added to the house, with a spacious slate terrace that overlooked the maturing garden. But during the hot summer months, the sun beat down, so an awning was added. However, the awning dripped water every time it rained and blocked the light that had given the sunroom its welcoming feeling. Clearly, the garden itself had come into its own, but an addition was still a work in progress.

In the early spring of 1996, Douglas and Billy Martin had a definitive meeting with the designer and contractor Steve Berg. Douglas produced a file overflowing with clippings and ideas for an ambitious, and what she hoped was a final, plan for a new outdoor structure. The addition would adjoin the backyard wing of their Flagg-designed home. Considering that Ernest Flagg is well known for designing the distinguished Scribner building on Fifth Avenue in New York City, the majority of the buildings at the United States Naval Academy, including the chapel, and the acclaimed Corcoran Gallery in Washington, D.C., it was important that any new plan blend with the spirit of the original design.

Douglas's carefully selected magazine clippings, as promising as spring tulips, provided a clear and useful way to communicate with the person who'd been asked to turn their personal vision into a practical plan—and to do it quickly, for the Martins' garden was listed on the Garden Club of Virginia's spring tour. Fanning out the glossy illustrations, Douglas explained how she and her husband were close to opting for a big porch—a space where they could linger over breakfast or sit in big chairs for hours without arising with chair lines pressed into their skin. "I told Steve it had to be a truly liveable out-of-doors place where we could sit well into the evening," Douglas said. The plan needed to provide an oasis for Billy and a perch for Douglas, always the vigilant gardener who can't resist jumping up to pull a weed or deadhead a flower.

Luckily, Steve Berg is a good listener, so when Douglas said "porch," he heard her describe a sheltered structure unblocked by screens or partitions, offering an uninterrupted view of the ever-changing scene in the garden. A plan unfolded on the spot for an open and spacious garden room under a protective roof and for a ceiling that was not flat or confining. They decided to use the footprint of the existing slate terrace for the foundation, a layout that had served the family well since 1984. That original terrace had been made the approximate size of two adjacent planting beds to add balance to the

ABOVE: Because the antique wire-and-wicker pieces are protected by a roof, the Martins can take a few liberties with furniture and fabrics. "There's always a risk that wire will rust in a blowing rain or that vintage fabrics will fade over the summer, but Billy and I believe in enjoying our wonderful finds for this extension of our home," Douglas explained. When it came to arranging the pieces in the new garden room for the first time, Douglas treated the space no differently from the comfortable and cozy living and dining areas inside her home. She's been known to change things around on a whim and enjoys interchanging indoor and outdoor accessories.

design. (Douglas's graceful perennial borders were mature and flourishing, and she was grateful she wouldn't have to move them so close to Virginia Garden Week to accommodate a larger terrace.) The existing flooring —local Virginia slate—required minor repair work and refitting. The final plan called for erecting the new structure directly over the terrace's outline, connecting it to the house at the point where the existing interior sunroom ended.

Steve Berg felt that the sunroom's low, flat roof was too long and "unaesthetic"—too modern—for the cottage-style dwelling. He wanted to vault up the new roofline, as Douglas had suggested, making it part of the original house and downplaying the adjoining flat roof. They decided on a classical half-pitch roof peaked on each side so it looks out to the view, installed with lighting and a paddle-style fan for added air circulation. When it came to the shingling, they selected a combination wood-and-composition material, a compatible match for the house's original roof. Painting the vaulted ceiling a soft "ocean blue" was Douglas's idea. "It's a traditional way of handling a porch roof, and I like the way it anticipates a nice day."

RIGHT: Douglas asked me to postpone photographing her new find—a charming Gothic wicker chair—until she could repaint it. I insisted that many people seek out pieces like this one that have been left in their original condition. Some months later, I was happy to find the chair in its virgin state. The unusual post next to the chair was given a playful addition when the gardener topped it with a wooden dove.

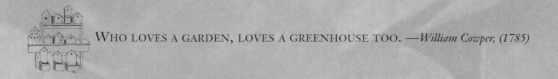

*An anonymous portrait of an unidentified Victorian garden room shows the
kind of breezy lifestyle that Douglas and Billy Martin hoped to emulate in their own garden
room. When it came time to make decisions about the design, Douglas pored over
her ample "idea file"—made up of miscellaneous photographs, magazine clippings, and
articles—to narrow down the many possibilities.*

Six classical Tuscan columns support the roof, a design derived from the Doric style, which mimics smaller columns used elsewhere in Flagg's original design. Everyone agreed that it made sense to use columns made of fiberglass, for these columns don't rot, can be found in proportionally correct sizes and styles, and are far less expensive and lighter in weight than traditional wooden columns. More important, they look authentic, even on close inspection.

The garden club visitors were scheduled to tour the Martins' garden less than a month after the start of construction. Early spring flowers were doing their job, but otherwise the clock was ticking. For three weeks, a handful of respectful workmen wore socks on the job as they tiptoed around budding hollyhocks rising from lush perennial beds. Additional supports were cantilevered over the plantings, and special scaffolding was erected for work on the cornices. Workers hung, quite literally, over the emerging blooms, close enough to catch the fragrance of the David Austin roses. The day before the garden tour, the garden room was ready for admiring visitors. It looked as though it had been there from the beginning.

Is this room the final chapter? Ask Douglas and she'll tell you about a new idea for a tin roof, painted an interesting green or, better yet, a vibrant blue—much like the sky that smiles on the Martins' garden.

RIGHT: A stone bird sits on the floor of the garden room.

LEFT: Lighting and a paddle-style fan for air circulation were part of a plan for creating a totally liveable space outdoors. Painting the vaulted ceiling a soft "ocean blue" is a traditional and pleasing way of handling a porch roof, and it works well in the deep space. "It anticipates a nice day," says Douglas of her choice of color. A table in the dining area was designed and hand-painted by the Atlanta artist Jane Keltner. The antique French cafe chairs keep the arrangement from looking heavy in the airy space.

ABOVE: A comfortable sofa, its painted iron frame dating from the 1920s, has been put to good and steady use since 1964, when Douglas acquired it. Douglas says she appreciates vintage porch furniture for its durability as well as its timeless design. The mix-and-match arrangement of pillows includes fabrics made of unique vintage florals, stylish traditional cottons, and one in needlepoint. Douglas likes to keep the upholstery of the furniture solid and neutral so that she can add color and interest with pillows.

THE PERFECT FOUNDATION
A Sunken Walled Garden from the Past

THE FIRST LIGHT of day had just begun to filter through a gauze of mountain mist on a sweeping ridge in one of the many remote valleys of western Massachusetts. Like a cat burglar, I made my way down a steep hill to a garden located at the base of the cliff-like drop just off the road. As soon as I reached the midpoint, I had a view of a place that embodied the purest definition of "garden room" imaginable—an unusual sunken garden, hedged by high

stone walls, that appears to have been inspired by the Roman Forum—after the fall of the empire. Immediately, I sensed a mystical aura, an unaccountable harmony, about this place.

The irregular stone structure is thick with climbing hydrangea, Virginia creeper, and wisteria. It's a sensitive study in blue and white—romantic peonies with blooms the size of mop heads, gentle flounces of amsonia, and a few hardy irises that have lasted into late spring, all gracefully combined with myriad shades of green and gray foliage that complement the blooms. There's an

PRECEDING PAGE: A view of the countryside through the original portals remains as it was when the Shaker community lived on the site. By keeping the doorways and window unblocked, the owners allow light to flow into the sunken room and breezes to circulate freely. The many full peonies were bowed by a recent storm.

ABOVE: The present owner recalls that her mother-in-law used to have afternoon tea at the millstone table when the garden was a more formal place. Today, full beds of perennials create low dividers for the sitting rooms.

attractive black iron dining set near a breezy portal and an old millstone that's been made into a small table. A circular bed planted with artemisia and campanula centers the space. It seems incredible that it has taken more than a century to coax the garden into its present serene state.

During the middle of the nineteenth century, a colony of Shakers—people given to a life of religious simplicity—lived on this same scenic ridge. Their twelve ample brick and frame-style buildings were clustered close to the narrow dirt road. Unfortunately, the Shakers lacked the means to sustain their modest settlement and the numbers of the faithful began to diminish. After their departure, three floors of one substantial dwelling were reconstructed across the neighboring valley, leaving behind the house's deep stone foundation. Finally, in 1885, the land and remaining dwellings were sold to people outside the Shaker community.

The new owners—a large, close-knit family—acquired the property as a retreat from city life. Respectful of Shaker ways, they took care to preserve any Shaker effects left behind. But, as fate would have it, the property changed hands again in 1907, when this family found itself hard-pressed to maintain it. Sadly, the property and all the remaining dwellings fell to a series of negligent owners and, eventually, to squatters. Then in 1927, in a happier twist of fate, descendants of the family that had originally bought the property in 1885 reacquired it.

The engaging story of the sunken garden begins when a most unusual garden was cre-

ated within the foundation of the Shaker house. "My mother-in-law was the first to create a garden in this ruin," the most senior of the present owners told me. She and her husband live in the tall brick house adjoining the garden. Recalling her very first visit to this place in 1954 as a new bride, she recounted: "It was a more formal space then, with fruit trees carefully tended by garden staff. I remember how my mother-in-law would always serve afternoon tea there, wearing a proper summer dress and a real hat." Today, with a more casual group of relatives and cousins living just a stone's throw from each other, the place has become an unassuming kind of family compound.

The present owners' interests in the garden and in history dovetail perfectly. He is a champion of Shaker heritage, active in preserving this significant part of American culture. She is the true keeper of the sunken garden, an artistic gardener who considers color, texture, and shape as a painter would when planning a still life. Inevitably, the garden has changed over the years, but not always by design.

The early Shakers had devised an effective drainage system using pipes that ran under the dirt road, taking water away from the main wall of the foundation. Many decades later, the town paved the road and the old drainage pipe was blocked. This caused a gradual accumulation of water behind the stone wall. Finally, the weight of the confined water caused the entire wall to collapse all at once. The owners arrived one weekend to find the floor of their garden and every

last flower buried beneath a heap of rubble. "It was a heartbreaking mess, but we turned it into an opportunity to redesign the space," said the gardener, with an admirable dose of New England optimism.

Generations of children have found adventure in this special place. So it was a reasonable step to recruit sons and daughters and a host of cousins to clear and sort the mountain of stones during their summer vacation. The job of rebuilding the wall took more than a year. A stonemason from Italy, aptly named Romulus (who even has a twin brother named Remus), matched the style of the other three walls, constructing occasional useful ledges around the original fireplace. When the work was completed, an empty expanse of hardy grass and the usual weeds were all that remained.

PRECEDING PAGES: A garden of small sitting rooms has been created within the foundation of an old Shaker dwelling. The space has gone from being a simple retreat with flowerbeds and a peach tree, to a heap of rubble (when the main wall collapsed), to an informal family gathering spot. The mysterious door at the far left originally led to the basement storage shed.

ABOVE: Due to blocked drainage pipes, the main stone wall weakened over a period of many years and eventually collapsed. This disaster required a new plan for the aged space, and in a relatively short period, a pear tree was espaliered there. Climbing hydrangea sets a rich green backdrop for the entire space.

FACING: The three-story brick house lies barely a step from a remote country road. There's an open kitchen garden below a stone retaining wall. The unusual sunken walled garden is located on the other side of the house.

The couple decided to create out-of-doors sitting rooms within the sunken garden—rooms divided by lush flower borders in an effort to keep the space from feeling too confined. A stone terrace was laid on one side to create a distinct space for dining. The durable millstone table was given an open view of the meadows and mountains beyond. A pear tree was espaliered on the reconstructed wall.

The sunken garden has become a world unto itself and, like a chameleon, it changes according to the occasion. The owners' grown children throw parties there now and enjoy the glow of torches dancing off stone walls. The youngest generation plays hide-and-seek behind mysterious doorways, as is the custom. A legacy filled with fascinating twists and turns has made this sunken garden even more meaningful to a family committed to its past as well as its future.

RIGHT: Modern life announces itself with a clean, straightforward pool that suggests a Shaker sensibility. Two simple terra-cotta pots at the far end of the pool hold the hope of more mature rosebushes next year.

FOLLOWING PAGES: The dining area has an airy view of long meadows and low foothills. When the main wall was rebuilt and the rest of the walls were repaired, a creative stonemason put in useful ledges for serving food or holding drinks—a sort of garden-room version of built-ins. The iron table and chairs are attractive and well-constructed copies of antique garden furniture ordered from the Winterthur catalog.

*This rare engraving, circa 1850, is taken from a stereopticon view of
the village where the walled garden flourishes today in the foundation of one of the
original dwellings. Active members of Hancock Shaker Village in Pittsfield,
Massachusetts, the garden owners are long-time collectors of Shaker antiques and
memorabilia. The engraving is from the museum's archives.*

California Magic
A Garden for Entertaining

CALIFORNIANS ARE MAGICIANS when it comes to transforming modest plots of land into estate-style gardens. Avid gardeners living in the central coastal areas benefit from a unique ecosystem in which they're able to grow an amazing variety of plantings with just the usual tricks of water, sweat, and soil. I'd heard tales of waist-high agapanthus and unbridled roses. So, in early July, I flew to the West Coast with my camera to see for myself.

A hillside garden near Santa Barbara has taken full advantage of such favorable conditions. The stucco house, a stylish blend of California and Provence, is tucked so discreetly behind a tall pittosporum hedge that I managed to drive right by it. Several sage-looking coastal California live oaks greeted me, their bark aged like weathered shingling. There's a fairy-tale enchantment in the way the knotty branches arch over the house, becoming part of the architecture. At once, I became a willing subject for this kind of illusion.

The one-acre property belongs to a couple who've recently retired from their regular routine, though they have hardly retired from their extended business and recreation-al activities, which are enough to keep ten people on the go. "We bought the house for the property's potential," one of the owners told me. Certainly "potential" is the operative word. Snapshots of the original bungalow make it look like a poor and distant cousin to the present house. Simultaneously redesigning the house and the garden was the couple's first major undertaking after moving to the West Coast from the eastern United States.

When they started on the garden, which was ninety percent cultivated at the time of my visit, it was little more than a sprawling back lot, filled with the area's basic vegetation—a natural habitat of cactus and other succulents, with a scattering of poppies, thanks to the birds. However, this Orange Bowl of a backyard, with sloping contours and graceful curves, suited the couple's needs perfectly. Whatever the occasion—their grown children visiting for the weekend with friends or a gala celebration for more than a hundred guests—they wanted visitors to be treated to a panoramic view of the entire garden and to have plenty of elbow room and comfort. Fortunately, a level stretch of ground at the crest, running from one end of the house to the other, provided the necessary space requirements. Today, anyone standing on the road in front of their property would hardly expect to find a backyard that resembles a luxurious retreat. With doors flung wide open and bugs either banished or sent back east, this home announces ever so naturally an indoor-outdoor lifestyle.

PRECEDING PAGE: A thriving espalier makes a capricious pattern of green on the stucco wall. "It's magnificent when it's in full bloom," the owners told me. The network of green is complemented with plantings of Japanese anemone and dusty miller; the window box is filled with bright impatiens.

FACING, TOP: There's jasmine, artemisia, and fern growing in the circular raised bed surrounding an oak tree. By taking advantage of the shelter offered by this wonderful old tree, the gardeners have a natural focal point for the terraced area as well, which is thoughtfully divided into a number of distinct conversational, dining, cooking, and lounging areas. Clearly, this is a garden created with entertaining in mind.

FACING, BOTTOM: The lap pool looks more like a sculptural reflecting pool, positioned inconspicuously at the far end of a spacious terrace near the main dining area. A recently constructed stone retaining wall adds interest to the view at the steep property line. The playful dog is waiting patiently for someone to fish his tennis ball out of the pool.

The land slopes naturally into a bowl, allowing a panoramic vista of the garden from the terrace. It's just one acre, but with ninety percent of the property devoted to the garden, and with many intriguing pathways leading to the wooded property lines, one has the sense of overlooking a rolling estate garden. A verdant patch of well-tended lawn offsets a magnificent rainbow of flowers, planted boldly so they don't get lost in the background. Contemporary wicker-and-iron furniture with thick, comfortable cushions speaks to California-style pampering.

ABOVE: There's a line of young fruit trees along one path, including fig, peach, Anna apple, and Santa Rosa plum, the latter of which is seen here. The newly planted roses in the arbor in the distance have just begun their climb.

Local sandstone flooring stretches from an inconspicuous lap pool to a more intimate area where the shade is the deepest. Contemporary wicker-and-iron furniture—made of a durable synthetic material that is easy to repair—has truly comfortable thick cushions, big ottomans for bare feet, and smartly placed end tables for refreshments.

The main conversational grouping is located only steps from the house's friendly family room and made even more inviting with a variety of sunny floral-motif pillows in vivid California-style colors. Coordinating chairs and a round glass-top table have been placed near a separate area designed for cooking outdoors. This cooking center is complete with a large gas barbecue grill and tiled slate serving surface. To pull it all together, the seating has been upholstered in a stain-resistant green cotton canvas, now softly sun-bleached, that coordinates with the soothing green trim of the house.

For the benefit of guests on the terrace, the avid gardener, a woman who serves as a docent for some of the area's private estate gardens and leads groups on garden tours, has painted the hillside with bold swatches of natural color. An arbor and the surrounding beds are devoted to countless roses; a breathtaking variety of perennials, including thousands of pincushion flowers and salvia, grow unrestrained on the hillside. The gardener has combined the more arid-loving plantings with her favorite herbs and flowers from gardening days back east—Boston ivy, bougainvillea, lavender, lantana, and prostrate rosemary. For a visual counterpoint to the flowers, and for games of boccie and croquet, the couple left a pleasing amount of lawn in the center of the garden.

There are the many pathways, several of which meander through thickets and give the impression of leading deep into the woods, when, in fact, they simply disappear at the property line. A wide composition walkway goes past a bench placed in a shady and meditative place; a narrow stone trail cuts between young fruit trees—plums, apples, and pears—some of which are ripe for picking. There's a bend in yet another path where the scent of jasmine is overwhelming.

ABOVE: One of many paths and walkways runs past a coastal California oak, looking much like a tree from the fairy tale of Hansel and Gretel, who surely would have been happy to rest on the stone bench beneath it.

Somehow I expected to find palm trees, but there's not one on the property. "They're phony and belong in Hawaii and Florida!" declared the non-gardener, who is happy to sing his wife's praises. He does, however, take credit for the wooden bridges that span a make-believe creek created with local stones gathered during the reconstruction project. The creek was dry when I visited, but it's fed by a nearby stream, and I'm told it can look like a raging river during El Niño, when nature displays its sorcery.

There's plenty of hocus-pocus in the exuberant trompe l'oeil painting on the white walls of a circular stairway inside the house. Its scenes depict the real thing outside in the garden: a bird on a familiar watering can, a basket of flowers, and, as always, the gardener's beloved roses in motifs repeated throughout the house. From the initial planning stages, a vital goal of this garden has been to provide flowers for cutting. Predictably, this gardener has containers to suit any occasion, including her treasured collection of richly colored majolica pitchers, one-of-a-kind pottery vases, and baskets.

I passed an arrangement of roses so perfect that I couldn't resist brushing my finger ever so gently across a petal—to make certain they were not simply part of the magic.

LEFT: There's a secluded nook where two old twig chairs have been given a fresh look with soft throw pillows covered in brightly printed fabrics.

FOLLOWING PAGE: Beyond the apple trees there's a bold sweep of roses.

IT IS NEVER TOO LATE TO LEARN THE PLEASURES OF PLANTING AND WATERING
A TREE, THE REWARDS AND VIRTUES OF HERBS AND PLANTS IN COOKING AND HEALING,
OR THE PLEASURE OF MAKING A BOUQUET OF FLOWERS. —*Charles Masson, 1994*

*The gardener has placed a writing desk close to double doors that remain wide open
to the garden, weather permitting, which is much of the year in this agreeable central coastal part
of California. The desk is strewn with jotted notes and things devoted to the garden. Every
morning, the gardener cuts flowers for the house, always playing favorites with the rose.*

BEYOND POTLUCK
Creative Instincts for Entertaining Outdoors

FOR KAREN SKELTON, having a special dinner for twelve friends can mean arranging bouquets from the garden in the graceful vases she creates at her own pottery (named PotLuck, which, clearly, it is not) as well as designing and throwing a dozen plates for the occasion. She does this in much the same effortless way that Richard Siegel, her husband, tosses and roasts salmon steaks on the grill, flavored with fragrant rosemary stalks brought back from a

trip to the South of France. If this couple's style is abundant, it's modestly understated at the same time, perhaps because they're motivated to create and not to impress.

It was just a casual dinner for the three of us on the evening I came to photograph their garden. A spacious deck overlooks a series of flourishing perennial beds—their American rendition of Monet's garden, with all the romantic favorites, such as purple allium, blue nepeta, and rose-colored peonies, and an abundance of lime-green foliage. I was flattered that the couple spared no attention to detail in showing me how it's done, yet no one stood on ceremony, so I sank back into the accepting curve of a wire-mesh garden chair. The fresh cotton table linens, softly folded right out of the dryer, complemented the earthy glazes of the dinnerware. There was a small wooden box with intricate dove-tailed corners, Zen-like in feeling, holding sea salt for diners to pinch, and the carefree flower arrangement on the table made me wonder why I never thought of combining hydrangeas with lady's mantle.

It took only three years for the couple, after they bought an 1845 farmhouse in New York State's lower Hudson Valley, a charming and rambling house-that-Jack-built kind of cottage assembled in stages, to develop a garden on their property, which had long awaited someone to care for it. There was barely a flower there then, not to mention a designated outdoor area for as much as a garden chair.

A stone terrace just outside the kitchen door offered hope for a cozy breakfast area.

The former owners had started a wisteria vine there for shade, but it was inadequate protection from the unrelenting midsummer sun. By raising a pergola over the entire terrace and training the wisteria, autumn clematis, and morning glory vines to shade the area, Karen and Richard had their first liveable space around which to begin a garden. To make it seem even more like an extension of the kitchen, they created a kitchen garden, filling out the perennial borders with bright nasturtiums, tall chives, plenty of healthy basil, and the many other cooking herbs they use on a regular basis.

ABOVE: A straight stone walkway makes a path through the main perennial garden to the arbor. It's given a regal introduction by urns filled with whimsical planting choices, such as pineapple and ornamental grasses. "I enjoy putting unusual perennials—grasses, ferns, hosta—in pots, then planting them in the earth in the fall," Karen Skelton pointed out.

The second real order of business was to install a spacious wooden deck on the far side of the house and French doors that would open onto it. Unfortunately, the new deck had a direct view of a large concrete slab that covered an old well. "With the basic ideas for our outdoor spaces either completed or at some hopeful stage," Karen explained, "Richard and I would sit out in the evenings watching the fireflies and making plans for our dream garden. And all the while, we'd be overlooking this terrible eyesore."

Together, Karen and Richard came up with the idea of a rose arbor. It would act as a

pleasing focal point, as well as a way to keep the garden from floating on a sea of rolling lawn. "At first, we were inspired to design a modern frame for the arbor—a Jennifer Bartlett-type house," Karen and Richard told me, making reference to the contemporary artist who's noted for painting houses in abstract yet familiar forms. Ultimately, they decided against this idea. "It might have been in keeping with our eclectic taste in art, but we decided that it was more important to respect the property's traditional character."

The lattice-style arbor—constructed directly over the well area—provided needed height on the property, was spacious enough for a pair of comfortable Adirondack chairs, and displayed a breathtaking flourish of old-fashioned roses entwined with autumn-flowering clematis. Not only does the arbor provide the focal point they needed, it adds a romantic air to the property as well. A straight stone walkway, framed by urns of unconventional potted plants—fountain

FACING: The chunky glasses—low-fired pottery with manganese and copper colorants—were picked up for five cents each in Mexico. The ruffled dinner plates and green spongeware salad plates are Karen's designs. A vase contains hydrangeas and lady's mantle from the garden.

ABOVE: Karen and Richard found a complete set of six molded wire-mesh garden chairs at a local antiques show. They've been unable to discover the chairs' specific provenance. However, judging from the strong and comfortable lines, they believe the chairs date from the late 1940s.

FOLLOWING PAGE: Future plans include moving an old barn, which presently crowds the house and the short driveway, to a new site on the other side of the property. There, a rerouted driveway will approach the house and garden in a more sweeping way. "We keep evolving," Richard declared, with true respect for the change and evolution that occur in the garden as well as in life.

grass and pineapples, eaten at the end of the season—invites visitors to take a stroll, then relax under a leafy ceiling.

Now the property has places to sit, spots to dine, and a swimming area that might be called rustic chic. "Do you *really* sit out under there?" I asked, with the diplomacy of Barbara Walters. Of course, I was referring to the idyllic arbor. The answer is that yes, they do indeed. In fact, it's one of their favorite places, a canopy of lush vines protecting them from the sun, the showers, and the bugs. And guests will continue to arrive, finding themselves simultaneously awed and relaxed in this creative setting.

WINTER IS ON MY HEAD, BUT ETERNAL SPRING IS IN MY HEART. —*Victor Hugo (1802-1885)*

This shot was taken on a cold February morning, barely five months
before the other photographs in this book and only hours before
one of the worst blizzards of the season. The area around the arbor is fenced off
during the winter months to protect the plantings from the hungry deer.
The perennials are cut back in the fall.

ABOVE: It was nice to have an existing pool on the property, located a short distance from the house, but until recently it seemed like little more than a charmless place to cool off—and yet another garden space to renovate and add to the couple's long list of priorities. Before the fence and classic wooden furniture were added, the pool looked too stark in such a bucolic setting. Surrounding the pool with bricks gave the area needed color and texture.

RIGHT: When it finally came time to build a rustic fence around the pool, in an effort to enclose and dignify the area, Karen happened to discover a flyer in their roadside mailbox advertising carpentry work. The ad was so effectively presented that she phoned the carpenter about the fence job right away, only to discover that he'd lost his job repairing copy machines in a recent downsizing. Going on instinct, Karen and Richard hired him for the job. Two years later, they enhanced his fine work by planting vines and climbers that add warmth and color to life around the pool.

A Life of Gardening
English Viewpoint, American Style

IT COMES AS no surprise that Margie Farinholt's personal vision of gardening dates back to her childhood, when she enjoyed playing outdoors in her family's garden on even the frostiest days. That garden was made up of engaging and distinct areas referred to by the gardening adults as "rooms." Margie remembers a formal bulb garden, where she watched for cheery signs of spring; a playhouse area with a cutting garden, where the flowers were hers to pick

without asking; and a vegetable garden, where Margie admits she pulled more excuses than weeds.

Many years later, in 1975, Margie bought a rambling clapboard house in a neighborhood where any hope of a level backyard and the garden rooms of her youth seemed to drop as abruptly as the steep slope only a few feet from the back door. The land's positive features included uncommon and sprawling vistas on two sides, plus a great and ancient holly tree. The tree towers over the back of the house, its wide sweep of branches acting as a protective canopy, keeping things cool

PRECEDING PAGE: Margie Farinholt designed a wooden archway that announces one of the primary pathways on her property. The finial functions as a sculptural element.

ABOVE: For more than two decades, Margie has been gardening her way from her house (far right) down a slope and over her property's steep terrain as she develops her personal concept of garden rooms—some for entertaining, others more intimate and confined. Since the property benefits from an expansive view of a golf course, it gives the sense of a much larger country estate.

even on the hottest summer day, which, in the state of Virginia, can be positively wicked.

Margie says the garden plan came to her during a routine moment familiar to most women—as she was doing the dishes. "Soon after we moved in," Margie told me over coffee in her friendly French-style kitchen, "I glanced out the kitchen window and decided I was tired of yelling for the children. I wanted to see my boys." One small revelation was all it took to come up with a flexible and appealing garden plan that would evolve to suit new needs and new times.

The first major step was the construction of a large, expansive wooden deck out over the knoll and around the great double-trunk holly, the unique shelter and beauty of which are impossible to duplicate. Several built-in benches around a generous floor area took care of the play space while at the same time providing an inviting place to sit and entertain more than a few adult friends. "The arborist who makes faithful visits twice a year to check on the tree appreciates how important and special it is to the property and to me," Margie emphasized.

After grading the land around the deck, Margie decided to develop terraced flower borders to camouflage the deck's tall support posts. From that spacious and functional main deck, other garden beds and liveable spaces followed in due course. Eventually, the deck was extended so that the family could benefit from the shade of another trea-

ABOVE: A recent addition, the garden shed is intended to be "almost like a garden sculpture to anchor the herb garden." The glass-paneled doors were found at a local salvage company. The whimsical cupola is an antique from North Carolina. A small cafe table and extra chairs are stored inside to expand the herb garden's entertaining capacity.

sured tree—a stately magnolia with waxy leaves the size of fans. Halfway down the shady north side of the house, the flooring changes from wood to slate, marking the beginning of a more formal outdoor dining area, bordered by boxwood on one side and mature azaleas on the other. A pleasant lounging area, covered by a large awning, is tucked closer to the house.

In 1988, when she acquired the adjacent house and small lot, Margie began to develop a series of meandering pathways to her new guest house and throughout the expanding garden—pathways that established needed connections among the various garden rooms. In 1998, a separate area for an herb

PRECEDING PAGES: The brick stairway, laid in a colonial Williamsburg pattern with treads braced by thick wooden ties, introduces another material to the property. This helps to unify the variety of materials used for walkways, pathways, and flooring. The wooden moon gate in the distance is a focal point, marking a verdant expanse of fairway.

ABOVE: "I wanted a formal dining area near the old trees, so I decided that the garden flooring should change from wood to slate to delineate the area," Margie explains. A large slate-top table is pushed close to a boxwood hedge until it's needed. Chippendale-inspired chairs carry out the more formal theme in this garden room.

FACING, TOP: The original backyard dropped down ten feet a short distance from the door, so the design and construction of a deck on graded and leveled land became a priority.

FACING, BOTTOM: The perfect spot off the kitchen for early morning coffee, this part of the deck is protected from the summer sun by an enormous magnolia tree. The wooden deck furniture has been selected for all the right reasons: rugged durability, classic lines, ageless appeal, and comfort.

FOLLOWING PAGES: Margie's garden has a cool, quiet pathway leading to a solitary room that feels like a secret from the rest of the garden. Pieces of slate have been laid in a circle around a sundial placed on an old balustrade. The stone bench—a cherished piece from the gardener's childhood garden—beckons.

garden and a garden shed were added and linked by a pebble path, and the different spaces became unified further. With her childhood memories intact, Margie looks forward to her pleasurable "morning coffee surveillance walks."

"I have been here for twenty-four years," Margie said. "In that time, I must have had a hundred birthday parties, countless Easter egg hunts, more than a few class parties, as well as bridal lunches and other celebrations in my garden." She's been open for Virginia Garden Week twice, too.

Perhaps because Margie, an antiques dealer, deals exclusively with things English, her garden has been profoundly influenced by British style. As she sits at a small table in the herb garden and adds to her list of things to do, Margie makes her points well. "With so many Americans, it's 'Snap! Let's have an instant garden!' The English are the masters because they're willing to give gardens time to evolve."

With so much going on, Margie needed a place for rest and reflection. To fill the bill, she found a deeply shaded alcove on a woodsy hillside. It required little more than a classical stone bench to make it into a private retreat. As I set up my camera and tripod in this solitary spot, I appreciated the patience it took for Margie to get to the point where she could enjoy the fulfillment of her vision for the garden.

WHAT IMPRESSED ME MOST ABOUT ENGLISH GARDENS WAS THEIR
GENEROSITY OF SPIRIT, AN EXUBERANT LAVISHNESS THAT COULD NOT ALWAYS
BE CONTAINED WITHIN STRICT SQUARES OR RECTANGLES. —*Susan Allen Toth, 1994*

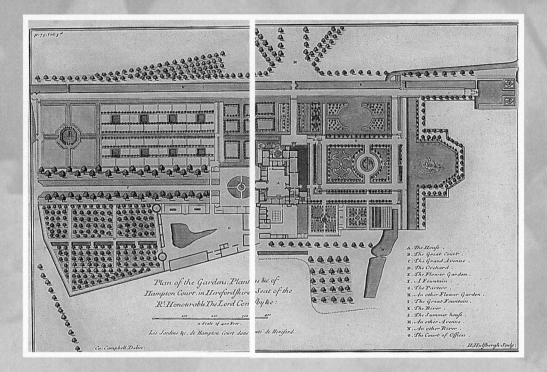

*The line between her role as gardener and her role as collector blurs when
Margie talks about her antiquarian garden prints and drawings, especially the exquisite
watercolor renderings of individual flowers and fine engravings of estate gardens.
An English hand-colored copper engraving, circa 1707, of the gardens of Hampton Court in
Herefordshire shows an amazing number of rooms. I'm awed by the
elaborate layouts," she commented, "as well as by the incomprehensible amount of work
it must have taken to maintain them. And the staffing!"*

NATURE AT ARM'S LENGTH
A Screened Garden House

THE TWISTY ROAD, with its endless dips and turns, is a kind of roller-coaster ride. Even without a map, I'd know I was in the foothills of southern New England from the very sense of the place. Perhaps the giveaway is a pristine clapboard church along the way, or the tall maples that line the roadsides and hillsides. Miles of dry stone walls amaze me for the labor it took to build them—but much more so for their art. The area's most distinctive feature, however,

is the succession of unsullied Colonial homes that sit close to the road, their rambling English cottage-style gardens a nod to the history of the area.

One summer day, I searched for one such landmark—a tidy 1738 dwelling long settled on a gentle hillside. During one neglectful time in the house's past, a tree had managed to grow through the roof; otherwise, the house has gotten through the years intact—without inept modernization.

It was fortunate that the former owners, who'd lived there since the 1920s, were

PRECEDING PAGE: "Family stuff," the garden owner said appreciatively of the bamboo-style chairs.

ABOVE: An original outbuilding was rebuilt in the same general style as the garden house, barely visible through the trees to the left. Now a storage shed, it holds a variety of furnishings and accessories for the garden house, a short walk away. "My idea to use a wonderful mishmash of terra-cotta pots was inspired by a stay at the Hotel Bel Air in Los Angeles," the garden owner told me. "I've never forgotten the way they plant a variety of the most cheerful flowers—geraniums, daisies, miniature carnations—in every pot, then plop them down everywhere."

ardent gardeners who gardened even more avidly during their retirement years. During this time, a fieldstone terrace was laid around a found millstone on a rise that overlooks the fields and woodlands behind the house. Until recently, perennial beds had spread in every direction, threatening to take over the entire side yard. There's a hedge of lilacs, planted in the 1930s and now reaching to twenty feet, that yields breathtaking flowers to cut and arrange every spring.

It might have been the perfect indoor-outdoor lifestyle for the new owners had it not been for the seasonal "guests" that made their lives a misery. Before I left, I had welty little souvenirs dotting my ankles, with a

ABOVE: A pair of silvery weathered wooden chairs make a seating area in the front yard of the house, enclosed by a neat picket fence. They provide a sense of welcome for people who happen to pass by.

fresh bite or two on the back of my neck. If this is paradise, it's even more so for the black flies and mosquitoes that give summer a bad name. The garden owners say they were tired of whipping plates and serving platters off the table in the middle of a meal or quickly marking passages in a book so they could dash for the safety of the house. They needed a plan to enjoy life in the country.

Before buying this house, the couple had rented a place with a screened structure on the property. It was a modest, fully protected camp-style building that had all the comforts of home—minus plumbing, which, according to the owners, "would have taken the relaxed intention of the building one step too far." It seemed to be the perfect place for living outdoors—in rain or shine and without nature's intruders—and the couple wanted to build something similar on their new property.

A dilapidated outbuilding located a convenient distance from the back of the house they bought had been put to good use as a storage shed. The land to the left of this building was open, offering the optimal spot for the new screened structure. They decided to build a screened room measuring twelve feet by eighteen feet—slightly larger than the rental inspiration—which would provide more space for entertaining.

The structure could be sited to take advantage of the prevailing western winds, assuring the owners of balmy afternoons and cool evenings and enabling them to sit out well after dark. In addition, powerful gusts and gales frequently whip through from the west, threatening to topple the gardeners'

RIGHT: I may have beaten the rising sun to get this radiant shot of the screened room, a freestanding garden house with picturesque views, but I didn't beat the mosquitoes, an especially ferocious lot in this part of southern New England. The cozy structure—a kind of compact studio apartment without plumbing—was constructed so that the garden owners could enjoy their property in all kinds of weather and on the buggiest days. From comfortable garden chairs just outside one of two doors, there's a view of the owners' 1738 Colonial house. Out of view is an essential, but otherwise unexciting, barbecue grill.

charming assortment of embellished terra-cotta pots and send them rolling across the lawn. The new building could serve as a substantial windbreak, replacing a nearby grove of pine trees that had grown too tall, rangy, and out of scale with the rest of the property to be effective.

An architect was called in to work on the construction details. Having lived on the property for five years, the garden owners had a good sense of the familiar footpaths and of the proposed building's comfortable minimum and maximum distances from the main house—a consideration when one is carrying food and dinnerware. They under-

ABOVE: In this modest twelve-by-eighteen-foot structure, there's room enough for a dining area, defined by a craftsmanlike table and benches, and a cozy living space. The dining area often expands to suit the guest list, with extra folding chairs and cushions stored nearby in the shed.

FACING: One side of the garden structure was designed to provide a solid wall for the sofa and also to hide the direct view of the storage shed next door. Light streams through the screened areas below the pitches in the roof. The decorative accessories include old tools and old signs. The tiny flowerpots hold candles.

stood what to expect from the various plantings that surrounded the site, in terms of the height, shape, and color changes that correspond to the changing seasons. Also, they knew that the view of the neighbor's field from this spot is as tranquil a vista as anyone could hope for. So locating the right site was a matter of familiarity and logic.

After the living area had been widened and enlarged from the original plan and other small modifications had been made, a cement slab was poured and construction began. Then came the news that the placement of so many long, screened windows only inches apart had weakened the framework. By shoring up the junctions with black iron corner braces anchored by steel, the problem was quickly corrected. Desiring a rustic feeling, the owners chose knotted pine for the exposed framing and rafters, and the cathedral-like ceiling added to the airiness of the room. In keeping with the casual, outdoors mood, the floor was made of brick. "It's not serious architecture," the garden owner told me unapologetically, "but it's well constructed and solid as a rock."

At the time the screened room was being constructed, the dilapidated outbuilding was demolished and replaced by a storage shed with a dirt floor and windows positioned on the sides and at the back. For the sake of compatibility, both the storage shed and the screened room were painted a fitting barn-red color. During the winter months, the long screens are replaced by wooden panels. Viewed from the house during the cold and bugless months, the two buildings have the appearance of twin barns. Now the storage shed holds the moveable feast of furniture for the garden room, including four benches and two pine-and-mahogany tables made by a local craftsman, folding chairs with cushions to seat twelve people, and the accoutrements for a barbecue grill located just outside one of the two doors.

Fond memories of summer camp came rushing back as we headed down a gentle incline toward the screened structure, far more upscale than my old Camp Tockwogh. A cozy living area is decorated with inviting country-style fabrics and personal treasures. There are useful hanging cupboards that hold silverware, glasses, and other practical things, including a good supply of candles.

Seated comfortably on a sofa upholstered in a fresh green-and-white check, I noticed dozens of small terra-cotta pots filled with candles, lined up along every shelf and every ledge. Then I spotted a hanging light in the center of the room—an incongruous note, given the spirit of such a rustic place. When I asked about the electricity, the garden owners assured me that they hardly ever switch on the lights. Instead, they prefer dining and reading by candlelight. Without a single winged creature to pester me, I took in a wonderfully gauzy view of the garden and the unfiltered sounds and smells of the country.

PRECEDING PAGES: Just outside one of the garden house's doors, a hammock beckons. Tall flowers have grown all around it. "You can see how often I have time to use it," the gardener lamented.

I HAVE STOPPED SLEEPING INSIDE. A HOUSE IS TOO SMALL, TOO CONFINING.
I WANT THE WHOLE WORLD, AND THE STARS TOO. —*Sue Hubbell, 1986*

*The garden's newly built screened room was inspired
by the warmth and the welcome of camp-like dwellings of the past, fondly
remembered for basic comforts and quiet contentment.*

DESPERATELY SEEKING SOLITUDE
A Cottage Porch and a Garden Dilemma

The unrelenting downbeat from a trendy downtown disco rumbling the walls of their New York City apartment at three o'clock in the morning was the final straw. Charles Muise and Gene Heil decided they'd had enough of life in the fast lane and began to search for a kinder, gentler place to live. They had but one simple need: a house with a peaceful yard and a small garden to call their own. Dreaming of Bach through an open window, they opted

for the small-town ways of a community in the Southwest, far from the bright lights and big city, where artists and retirees like themselves might find a refuge. There they found the perfect 1940s cottage, and there the story of their escape from the frenzied city should have ended. But the street ran brazenly close to their property line, separated from the pleasant front porch by a mere twenty-four feet and a parched patch of crabgrass. The land bordering the back of the cottage dropped off so precipitously into a deep ravine that it offered no solution to their garden dilemma. Tranquillity continued to elude them.

PRECEDING PAGE: There is little room in the yard for grand ornamentation, which would make the space seem even more crowded, but a simple round birdbath with a permanent visitor serves as a focal point just off the porch. Every year, it's bordered by bright pansies that benefit from the splashing.

ABOVE: The original and unalterable size of the yard in front of the house was exactly sixteen feet wide by fifty-nine feet long. The street lay only twenty-four feet from the front porch. Poor soil filled with limestone and a blistering southern exposure might have been okay when the space was used as a parking spot for the former renters, but for the owners it needed a plan to look like home. Building a natural picket-style fence—high enough for privacy but low enough for neighborly chats—was the first step in creating a more intimate space. Tall flowers, such as foxgloves (see closeup on facing page), hot pokers, and Shasta daisies, soften the fence line.

Soon, Charles and Gene came up with a plan to build a natural picket fence (a timeless look that requires very little maintenance) close to the road for privacy. A gate would go on the street side in line with the porch steps. At the same time, they'd lay a dry stone wall about a foot from the fence on the road side—a low wall that even short flowers could peek over. Building the fence close to the road seemed to make perfect sense, since the quiet dead-end street was used mostly by neighbors with a destination in mind, usually home. With installation only days away, they discovered that the local zoning code required any fencing to be built outside the long-abandoned sidewalk line. Unfortunately, the phantom sidewalk was actually in their planned front yard. "Fighting long-established zoning laws, even on a little street like ours, is like fighting Mother Nature," Gene told me. "If we wanted our garden, we had to work with both!"

With a stream of curious new neighbors leaning over the fence in a helpful, down-home way, Charles and Gene filled in the narrow strip of ground between the fence and the porch, then leveled it. The soil was rich and the sunny location was perfect for perennials—tall foxgloves planted irregularly along the fence line on the road side for added privacy; Shasta daisies, with their cheerful faces; a scattering of hot pokers for an eccentric burst of red; tall canna near the living-room windows for shade and privacy.

Every spring without fail, Charles introduces an exotic plant that quickly becomes a conversation piece. I can imagine the locals

ABOVE: An ordinary white plastic lawn chair—attractive, comfortable, and inexpensive—gets a bit of padding with light-weight cushions. Because Oliver, a spoiled new puppy, made short work of a few tie strings, the cushions are sometimes held down on gusty days with old-fashioned clothespins.

RIGHT: The homeowners rose to the occasion when they created an inviting porch space on a modest budget. By hanging a friend's bright oil painting on the wall of the house and tossing a well-worn woven rug on the concrete floor, they made the porch homey. By filling a newly painted poultry feeder with bougainvillea, they created a low barrier across the front, delineating the porch space. "The large urn is our one delusion of grandeur," commented Charles Muise.

BELOW: A weathered footstool on the porch is nice when you want to put up your feet; nice in the garden when you want to pot things sitting down.

ABOVE: "Sometimes it's best to work with what you've got," Gene Heil said when he told me about the precipitous slope on the far side of the house that quickly drops into a ravine. Filling and grading this area for a terrace are part of the owners' future plans. For the time being, they dress up the yard with another colorful pot.

cool on the modest concrete porch, which cries out for catnaps and leisurely dinners. "At that point, we had more taste than funds for a porch project," Charles told me as we enjoyed shivery glasses of old-fashioned lemonade on an unseasonably warm spring day. "As it turned out, our solution of matchstick roll-up shades was both attractive and downright cheap." Today, a shade hangs between the porch railings on both sides of the steps. Another one hangs inside on the big living-room window, keeping the house cool throughout the day.

With the second big problem solved, the rest was easy. Charles found charming interior accessories to use out-of-doors: a bright oil painting done by a friend to hang on an expanse of exterior wall; a pleasantly faded woven rug to toss on the concrete floor.

"There were more expensive solutions," Charles mentioned. "But this is really all we need to enjoy our porch and be near the garden." All in all, the porch had become a cozy room and an extension of their home.

The porch is perfect for three; cozy for five. As we sat and enjoyed the fruits of their labors, I adjusted the back cushion of my comfortable chair—white molded plastic that's practically indestructible. "They're light as a feather," Charles said cheerfully. "So if we're on the porch when we get a twister warning, we can just grab our chairs and head for low ground!"

It struck me then that a noisy disco might not have been so bad after all. But the air was still on that lazy afternoon and the little porch felt like peace at last.

saying to each other, "Wonder what these city guys will come up with this year." One year, it was a chandelier plant; the year before, a castor bean plant. Many of the neighboring gardens are bigger, but this cottage garden has won all the votes as the most popular, as well as the most original.

The southern exposure is perfect for the perennials, but the porch can become a hot zone during the summer months. The next major challenge was staying private and

WE GO TO THE COUNTRY BECAUSE WE ARE TIRED OF THE TOWN; AND
WE HOPE TO FIND THERE, NOT A SECOND OR THIRD-RATE REPRODUCTION
OF WAYS OF LIFE WITH WHICH WE ARE WEARILY FAMILIAR, BUT
SOMETHING NEW AND DIFFERENT—CHANGE, REST, AND QUIET, REFRESHING
COMMUNION WITH NATURE, AND A MODE OF LIFE LESS ARTIFICIAL THAN
A CITY EXISTENCE MUST OF NECESSITY BE. —*Margaret E. Sangster, 1904*

*To come up with a garden plan for the narrow and barren strip that separates his and
Gene Heil's 1940s cottage-style house from the street, Charles Muise sketched ideas and jotted
notes on sharp computer-generated copies of snapshots of the house and front yard as
they originally looked. This offered a quick and helpful way to visualize the stone wall and fence,
where tall flowers—hot pokers unnamed flower and foxglove—would be planted.
"I like being able to see the site and experiment with different solutions on surfaces I can toss
out until they look right," Charles explains.*

THE GARDEN PATHS TAKEN

Green Links Among Family and Friends

WHEN CYNTHIA AND KIRK DUPPS say, "Just make yourself at home!" they mean it. Without further prompting, I left my urban stress on the breezy front porch of their log home in the Ozark Mountains. Until 1994, the couple lived in a large, formal house with a small yard and minimal landscaping ("the basic trees and shrubs in the suburbs") and wondered if the grass might be greener on the other, more rural, side. When they took the plunge and

built a decidedly more modest and rustic home, they were rewarded with two and a half acres of glorious, rolling green fields, their own private cove on Table Rock Lake, tall cedar trees that form an umbrella over the house, and a rugged wilderness view. Wild turkey, deer, foxes, wild rabbits, and raccoons are kept at bay by two intrepid cats and a noisy dog.

The main residence of the place they've named Cedar Cove is a straightforward log-style house. It boasts a put-your-feet-up kind of comfort, yet this is no simple cabin in the woods. It takes a while to realize that the Duppses have given country style a unique infusion of sophistication and whimsy. Rooms filled with artisan-created pieces and artful arrangements also grace a nearby garage-turned-guest-house, as well as a one-room fishing cabin affectionately called Standing Room Only. Once they had put together this small compound of buildings for family and friends, the couple needed a garden to link and unify the various structures. With the exception of a few irises, nothing had ever been planted on the property.

The flourishing garden started its life as a gravel driveway leading right up to the front door. Cynthia and Kirk may have been novice gardeners, but they were determined to go at it without professional help. It doesn't take an expert to know that successful outdoor living spaces need more than a few

PRECEDING PAGE: Cynthia and Kirk Dupps have created unique porch railings from pine branches with the cones still attached which they collected on their property.

ABOVE: There is much that is woodsy on their property, which is why Cynthia and Kirk decided to go for a kind of decorative counterpoint by choosing a white trellis-style iron bench—newly made and easily moved—for the front garden.

FACING: Ordinary garden tools offer such simple sculptural beauty that Cynthia and Kirk prefer to keep them in clear view.

FOLLOWING PAGES: When Cynthia and Kirk abandoned a suburban lifestyle in favor of a more rural existence, they built a log house in the country and began to create a compound of small dwellings for their family and friends. A 1940s fishing cabin, seen in the distance, was moved to the property.

chairs and magnificent distant vistas. To arrive at a plan that represented their personal vision, the couple first looked at other people's ideas—in magazines, books, catalogs, and garden encyclopedias—and solicited advice from local nurseries and friends in the landscaping business.

Together, Cynthia and Kirk graphed out the entrance by the front porch on paper, sketching in the different beds and the arrangement of furniture. They worked the planting beds by hand. In no time at all, their interior style had spilled across the thresholds, onto the porches, and into the garden. Their taste in flowers and shrubbery began to settle on favorite colors and combinations. "Enthusiasm, perseverance, muscle, and sweat got us through this project," Cynthia told me. As I felt the rising summer heat, I knew that there must have been more than a little sweat.

The use of local natural resources is apparent, especially in a unique porch railing made and designed by Kirk from cut pine branches, the miniature pine cones still attached. Local stone has been used for the steps leading to the house and various pathways. Loose stone paths play a major role in connecting the main dwelling with the other distinct spaces. The whole plan is deceptively simple, yet it manages quite happily to facilitate the flow of house guests and party guests, providing a kind of self-guided tour of the property.

Cynthia says she is constantly moving potted flowers from one place to another. A gardener who follows her heart, Cynthia loves

FACING: The rustic porch cried out for the right furniture—fortuitously found on a trip to Michigan, where an Adirondack-style resort lodge, dating from the 1940s, was selling its furniture. The right decorative touches include old fire buckets planted with bright annuals and hung at intervals, a red-and-black throw blanket for chilly nights, a carved wooden beaver to guard the doorway, and elk antlers hung over the benches.

ABOVE: Using a nail, Cynthia punched a hole at the tip of her old fire buckets for drainage. Each year, she plants them with different annuals, and always with ivy to trail. "The plants don't dry out as quickly as you'd think," says Cynthia, who loves the buckets' soft, timeworn finish.

FOLLOWING PAGES: Cynthia came up with the idea of pine branch porch railings because she wanted a railing that would go with the look of her outdoor furniture. Kirk found branches in the nearby woods and then brought them home to air dry. Cynthia and Kirk arranged the loose branches to fill the spaces between the existing pine posts. Finally, the branches were nailed and screwed to each other and to the posts, and a polyurethane finish was applied for all-weather protection.

reds and other vibrant colors and frequently uses colorful punches of red geraniums, hot-pink begonias, and deep purple lavender to enliven the garden.

Kirk wound up as the guest of honor at a recent November birthday party held for him and two friends. The porches are narrow, so Cynthia used folding conference tables there, decorating them with sporty checked tablecloths. Since all three men are avid trout fishermen, she filled paper minnow buckets with spider mums and cattails. Buckets, old crocks, fishing creels, and antique bread tins served as the meal's serving pieces. A metal canoe filled with ice kept the beverages frosty.

I can imagine guests strolling from one delightful interest area to the next, exploring the Duppses' rustic compound, which was inspired by a dramatic change in lifestyle that perfectly suits both the gardeners and the garden.

LEFT: Cynthia has a special fondness for the tall and colorful *Malva*, which she and Kirk planted along the fence in front of the house.

FACING, TOP: Because their home is small, the Duppses have transformed the garage into a charming guest cottage for their two daughters and the many visitors who find their way to this part of the deep woods. The split-rail fencing, a theme on the property, sections off a comfortable seating area filled with decorative touches, including a birdhouse from New England placed on a pedestal. Ornamental trees and shrubs include a Japanese maple tree, boxwood, and, as always, red geraniums.

FACING, BOTTOM: For the guest house, Kirk constructed porch railings and matching decorative brackets from air-dried pine branches, just as he did for the porch of the main house.

EVEN YOUR OWN GARDEN DOES NOT BELONG TO YOU. RABBITS AND BLACKBIRDS HAVE THE LAWNS; A TORTOISE-SHELL CAT WHO NEVER APPEARS IN DAYTIME PATROLS THE BRICK WALLS, AND A GOLDEN-TAILED PHEASANT GLINTS HIS WAY THROUGH THE IRIS SPEARS. —*Anne Morrow Lindbergh, 1938*

Now that Cynthia and Kirk Dupps are converts to cabin-style living, they snap up wonderful old souvenirs that remind them of home. A hand-colored copper-plate etching, circa 1796, shows a wild ride on a swing from a bygone time. "It has the new ones beat by a mile," said Kirk.

PRECEDING PAGE: The red metal chair, one of two, was given a new life when a floral motif was painted on the back in acrylic paint, then spray-varnished after the paint had dried completely. To ensure that the finish of the chairs will last, the Duppses make sure to pull them under the roof's overhang in bad weather and take them indoors during the chilly months.

ABOVE: A child's antique pine sled wears many hats throughout the year. Sometimes, it goes inside the house, where it plays host to a potted fern, a Christmas tree, or pumpkins. In the summertime, it stays on the porch, where it shows off an array of geraniums and a pot of daisies set to one side.

RIGHT: Cynthia designed this clever fish smoker and cooker for Kirk as a surprise birthday gift and had it fabricated by a local welder.

BLOOMS AND COUNTERPOINT
Finding Roses and Paradise in a City Setting

AS SOON AS I ARRIVED to photograph a brownstone rose garden in New York City's Greenwich Village, my attention shifted to the owners' rambunctious Siamese kitten named Digger Roo (a playmate for Tigger Too), who calculated that an escape through my legs was the quickest route to the tempting wilderness beyond, where thousands of rosebuds had burst into full bloom. Lemeau Arrott-Watt, a transplanted Australian, has worked and

nurtured this stubborn plot for fifteen years with her Maryland-born husband, Richard Duckett. As she fussed tenderly at Digger Roo, she was very quick to tell me that the yard was a far cry from paradise when they moved in.

The couple's typically modest city yard runs fifty feet from the kitchen door to a far fence that faces south, where the land has been pleasingly terraced into a comfortable dining area, complete with a traditional brick barbecue, essential for Australian-style entertaining outdoors. High split-log cedar fencing, unobtrusive and pleasantly weathered, confines the space on the other two sides. The effect is that of a small paradise, complete with little rooms that are given

PRECEDING PAGE: Garden ornamentation, such as the faux-lattice stone planter, remains in harmony with the tone of the furniture while adding a charmingly busy touch.

ABOVE: This twenty-by-fifty-foot city garden—boasting a breathtaking variety of roses—was created in levels and is spatially deceptive. The design of the site was an ultimately rewarding trial-and-error project, requiring rethinking and reworking as the needs of both the human and the botanical occupants evolved. Over time, the people moved to the shade; the flowers got the sun. Indeed, every sunny nook and cranny is planted with blooming things, such as hydrangeas and clematis, and, of course, roses: floribundas and grandifloras fill the middle heights, climbing roses rise to greet the neighbors. The simple and classic wooden furniture is comfortable and durable and doesn't compete with the colors in the garden.

cozy privacy by magnificent mature stands of roses, well-established hydrangeas, and low perennials, which add richness and color in their seasons. It's such a beautiful and successful city garden that I have trouble imagining it looking any other way.

Growing up outside of Melbourne, Lemeau recalls feeling like "a lump on a rock" as she watched enviously while her mother and sister gardened together. "They simply had the knack, and I did not," she declared in a no-nonsense tone. Lemeau's passion for gardening came years later, when she and Richard moved into their present home. A ground-floor apartment in a large old residential brownstone, it came with what the sellers optimistically called a garden: a bleak and run-down plot in which the only positive feature was light—it had a southern exposure and was surrounded by low buildings that allowed for unblocked light all day long. Even this was enough to excite the couple, who together possess a good eye for design, a strong will, and a desire to enjoy leisure hours in their own backyard.

A classical English garden design—a central circle with grape arbors at opposite points—inspired the evolving plan. But first, a sixty-four-foot tree at the plot's dead center, which shaded the entire area—pleasant for people, but hardly an asset for a flower garden—had to come down. Then there was the sea of old slate.

"A ten-pound hammer and a crowbar became my best friends," Lemeau said as she described how, single-handedly, she broke up slabs of slate that covered most of the yard to make way for paths of old brick and brick borders for the new beds of roses and perennials. "When I got to the raised terrace at the far end, I simply buried the huge slate under fresh topsoil," she said victoriously.

Soil that Lemeau wanted to replace with sand to set the old bricks in place presented another challenge. So, week after backbreaking week, giant-size trash bags of earth were hauled to the stoop for the regular garbage pickup. Soon thereafter, a shipment of fifteen hundred old bricks, delivered to the sidewalk in front of the brownstone and unceremoniously dumped there, was carted through the brownstone apartment to the site. Lemeau—a delicate woman, not an Amazon gardener—borrowed a cart from her local grocery store and began another of her many labors of love.

Fifteen years later, it is a different space entirely, but it is not the perennial garden that Lemeau had imagined. After what she describes rather playfully as "the war of the roses," Richard's passion for roses won out. Now, central quadrants are filled with an array of English and antique roses—shrub roses, floribundas, grandifloras, and climbers—and the garden thrives. The roses are balanced with perennials in beds along the fences and planted within the rose beds for fullness. When Lemeau and Richard could finally concentrate on outdoor furnishings, they knew they needed pieces that would work in their small jewel of a space in the middle of Manhattan. "An inch is a mile when you're dealing with space in New

PRECEDING PAGES: The original backyard plot was paved with untold pounds of weighty slate, which the owners moved piece by piece to the borders and walkways. When the project reached an upper level at the farthest point of the plot, Lemeau says she was happy to be able to bury the slate with topsoil to make room for a dining area and plantings. The off-center walkway provides space on one side for seating and on the other side for a full garden bed.

ABOVE: The classical lines and substantial proportions of this stone garden urn—one of several in the garden—provide a focus as well as an element of drama.

FACING: Lemeau grew up in Australia, where a yard wouldn't be complete without a place to dine and have a barbecue. The round table and simple green cafe chairs are casual in design and easy to move.

York," said Lemeau with authority, donning her professional cap as an interior designer. "And you cannot waste any of it."

The couple decided to go with French cafe furniture for the dining area—a green metal table with folding chairs. With little room to store pillows and fragile accessories, they deemed other types of furniture impractical. The seating area in the center of the garden is made up of softly weathered teak pieces. These aesthetically pleasing choices stand up to the elements year-round.

Lemeau characterizes ceilings as forgotten spaces in the modern world and enjoys "the gift of God's skies and clouds as nature's ceiling." She designs her own spaces, indoors and outdoors, in layers—from the floor to twelve inches above it, then from twelve to thirty-six inches, then from thirty-six to fifty-four inches. It's a useful formula that provides layers of texture and color. When you walk through these garden rooms, you find no awkward spaces, no bloomless voids.

On the day of my visit, news of Frank Sinatra's funeral was splashed across the headlines. As if out of the blue, "It Was a Very Good Year" drifted from an open window next door, punctuated by the muffled sound of a banging door and an intermittent clanking of pots and pans across the way. I was also aware of someone practicing scales at the music school at the end of the block; as if on cue, a well-trained soprano hit all the high notes of a lilting aria.

Rather than a fight for urban air space, a magical contrapuntal symphony is under way in Lemeau and Richard's hard-won paradise.

MEMORY IS THE POWER TO GROW ROSES IN WINTER. — *Anonymous*

During the winter months, a vase of hothouse roses and an
array of objects bearing various rose motifs, including framed prints
and drawings, remind Lemeau Arrott-Watt
and Richard Duckett of their town house rose garden.

Form Follows Function
A Spontaneous One-Room Garden Plan

THERE'S AN ELM, a Cedar, and a Walnut. The serene and timeless street names of a Long Island, New York, village—its residents never call it a town—evoked images of wraparound verandas and antique roses. When I visited a garden there, I was hardly disappointed. As I searched for a century-old Victorian home, I envisioned snowy-haired ladies sipping iced tea spiked with long sprigs of mint fresh from the garden.

Judi Boisson, however, is a dynamic twentieth-century woman all the way. When I arrived, she was busy planting daisies and sprucing up a modest corner of her nineteenth-century paradise. The phone—a shared line with her business, located a quick drive away—rang loudly and continually from inside the house. There were stacks of little plastic pots, fresh dirt still clinging to the sides, and gigantic empty bags of topsoil left

in a heap near a unique and welcoming garden fence designed to resemble an American flag. I held on to my hat as I ducked under the lowest branch of a great-grandfather sort of Canadian spruce near the gate.

"My garden's a mess!" Judi declared, which is what every gardener I interviewed for this book told me. "I feel terrible that the rhodies aren't cooperating!" Then she gestured in the direction of tall rhododendron bushes only a few days away from their yearly splendor. Aside from a hard rain that had left azalea petals sprinkled over the garden like hot-pink confetti and an isolated parched area on the spacious lawn, where Judi attempted to zap a few stubborn weeds, her backyard garden was picture perfect that day.

When Judi bought this property in 1984, she was not a person to be put off by an unremarkable backyard the size and shape of a tennis court, planted "smack in the middle" with two holly trees, a pear tree, and one mature azalea bush. "Up until the day I bought the house, I actually thought the yard ended there," she told me, pointing to a stretch of lawn where the original plantings had stood before they were moved to more suitable spots. "When I discovered I owned a wide strip behind the trees as well, it was like a bonus!" Still, it remained an underdeveloped space without personality and without a plan.

In the beginning, it was the porch that drew her in. ("Just find me a wonderful house with an old-fashioned porch," Judi told the real estate broker.) The wide porch, which hugs two sides of the living room, is shaded by old trees and kept cool and private by a high hedge of boxwood and euonymus. Even though the house is separated from the sidewalk by only a narrow band of lawn, the fact that there are few pedestrians and even fewer passing cars makes it feel more like a refuge.

Judi uses an inviting mix of new textiles—her richly colored quilts and floral rugs—on an eclectic collection of granny-style wicker porch furniture from Alabama that has true southern charm. Judi has gracefully broken up the space into a number of comfortable seating areas, adding to the welcoming feeling. Lush green ferns spill from planters and bright geraniums hang in baskets. It's a cozy porch with whimsical touches that make you want to put your feet up with a good book or settle into all those comfortable pillows for a nap.

Some new homeowners might have been frustrated by the plot-like space in the back with close neighbors on all sides, but Judi relished the idea of having so much lawn to work with. Nonetheless, it took many passing seasons and a wealth of spontaneous ideas, not to mention two thousand cubic feet of topsoil, to bring the backyard garden up to speed. During this time, Judi held on to a vision of the backyard as one enormous room with plenty of space for her collection of outdoor furniture, which can be easily moved to make room for a badminton net or a game of croquet. When it comes to exterior design, it's always been a case of form follows function for Judi, who explains, "I find a tree that's full or a bed that's glorious, and I think

ABOVE: A wicker swing is in tune with the porch's grandmotherly mood, but it's dressed up with a colorful pillow done in a bold folk-art style. Rugs, such as this newly hooked throw rug, create cozy gathering areas. The potted palms are moved inside the house during the winter months, as are the ferns.

RIGHT: There was plenty of floor space for a living-room arrangement at one corner of the porch, and the old wicker sofa was positioned at an inviting angle. With a new needlepoint rug warming the floor, comfortable chairs to sink into, and potted ferns and geraniums adding to the charm, the porch has become the quintessential old-fashioned porch room.

FOLLOWING PAGES: Judi has held on to her original vision of the backyard as one enormous space—a kind of great room. Well-worn Adirondack chairs, arranged in a friendly grouping, create a comfortable and functional seating area. When the guest list expands, extra chairs are brought up from the basement and placed here or moved to another part of the lawn. A dining area to the left features durable wrought-iron furniture. In the distance, two well-spaced benches hint at more solitary moments.

ABOVE: There's a second dining area set up in front of a
converted barn near the pool. When the wisteria is in full
bloom, this is Judi's favorite spot to entertain. The vintage
painted-iron furniture with its decorative floral motif adds to
the visual variety of the furniture used throughout the spacious
yard and garden. On the day of my visit, Judi tossed a newly
made quilt over a glass tabletop. She commented, "I love
using unlikely textiles for the table if they can be laundered."

BELOW: There's a sense of whimsy in one quiet corner
of the yard, where a nineteenth-century folk-art weathervane
sits atop a stone birdbath-turned-planter. The corner
arrangement is completed by an iron bench dating from
around 1920.

how nice it would be to sit down there. So
I'm always changing things around—furniture, pillows, tablecloths."

When the neighbors decided to sell a
small barn on the adjoining property—a sou-
venir of nineteenth-century farming in this
area—Judi found herself the fortunate buyer.
Its move several yards across property lines
gave her the perfect guest house/pool house,
next to which Judi constructed a pool—at
the far end of the yard, away from the main
house. Although the barn retains its original
exterior charm, the interior was completely
rebuilt to accommodate the needs of
modern-day guests.

In the yard, a circle of weathered Adirondack chairs in a sunny spot seemed posi-

tioned for good conversation. There are two wonderful antique cast-iron benches, both in pleasant shady areas, waiting for couples and solitary moments. There's a dining area set up near the pool and another one off a small back deck that leads to the kitchen.

"My guests look forward to being a part of what's going on, but even in this modest space, they know they'll have solitude if they want it." All this is Judi's version of a moveable feast in the garden.

ABOVE: The small barn was located on a neighboring property until Judi bought and moved it. Because the exterior of the old structure was in good condition, it has retained much of its original charm and has made few concessions to the twentieth century. On the other hand, the interior required a complete renovation before it was qualified to win the four-star praises it now commands from the many guests who enjoy it. The small structure lies only a short distance from the house, yet a sense of privacy is retained.

WITH ITS PROMISE OF BLUE SKY DAYS AND STARRY NIGHTS, SUMMER IS THE SEASON WHEN WE TRADE THE COCOON OF OUR HOME FOR THE FREEDOM AND COMFORTS OF THE FRONT PORCH. —*Ann Rooney Heuer, 1998*

Tome VIII. *Pl. 7.*

ORNEMENTS DIVERS *Fabrique de Puntz à Metz* (Moselle.)

If her wonderful old drawings of garden furniture are tucked into manila files instead of chunky albums, it's because Judi Boisson collects them for a practical reason. She uses the sources as inspiration when designing garden-furniture models for her business.

The Changing Face of a Garden
Playing to Spectacular Borrowed Spaces

Perfectly manicured lawns are de rigueur and all hedges are high and well trimmed in an established neighborhood on the outskirts of this small southeastern city. So when a certain gracefully contoured two-and-a-half-acre property began to grow untidier by the season, it seemed an obvious indication of either poor manners or an approaching sale. The still elegant but sadly neglected 1920s Georgian-style house was showing its age when

Pattie and Mason Williams, college sweet-
hearts who'd grown up nearby and were raising a family, bought it in 1992.

Their inherited garden displayed little
more than a lingering sense of its original
plan by the noted garden designer Charles
Gillette. Instead, a shaggy assortment of
American boxwood loomed like woolly mam-
moths, and most of the shrubbery had been
overtaken by wild interlopers from other
yards. A jungle of honeysuckle that separated
the house from a potentially spectacular view
made the entire garden look as though it had
fallen under a Sleeping Beauty-like spell.
Pattie Williams claims it was her husband,
Mason, who became the garden's enchanted
prince, rescuing it from azalea bushes grown
thick and awkward along the driveway, huge
and shedding magnolia trees, and a substantial unplanted area of yard in the back that
resembled a vacant lot.

Pattie Williams swept open tall French
doors off the living room and I followed her
onto a spacious terrace. All around lay evi-
dence of a fondness for things Jeffersonian
that I've come to anticipate in his native

PRECEDING PAGE: Pots planted with miniature roses
and pink geraniums complement the colors of the floral-
patterned cotton fabrics.

RIGHT: Sometimes a classic scene will present itself
flawlessly to the camera's eye. Certainly this was my
experience with the Charles Gillette-designed brick pool and
fountain, which I photographed on a day when the late
afternoon light was the pleasing color of sweet creamy butter.
The mature American boxwood has created an evergreen
room, a solitary place where a cast-stone bench seems a
welcome throwback to a less stressful era.

ABOVE: The garden of a 1920s Georgian-style house had been allowed to languish for many years before a hometown couple—both the husband and the wife grew up nearby—bought it in 1992. Working in bold strokes, Pattie and Mason Williams cleared away the brambles and thickets, opened up the overgrown vistas, and saved much of the abundant American boxwood to make way for a garden that feels like home. The first order of business was replacing a number of windows on the back of the house with doors—tall single doors as well as graceful French doors—all of which open onto a new stone-and-brick terrace.

state. The terrace overlooks raised beds planted with symmetrical globes of boxwood on a ground cover of ivy, given shape by a brick retaining wall. It seems incredible that the original house had no doors opening onto the back property, no flat expanse of outdoor living space, and no flowers growing on such lovely undulating terrain. As the Williamses worked to restore the house, they made access to the evolving garden an intrinsic part of the plan. Today, the elevated vista is of an uninterrupted and panoramic expanse of lawn—the rolling fairways and greens of a neighboring country club and golf course. Earlier, the view of this spectacular and verdantly serene borrowed space had been blocked by the infamous honeysuckle bramble.

As I settled into a comfortable deck chair and took in how tranquil—not to mention how perfectly realized—this garden is, Pattie spoke about how she and Mason came up with a plan to establish a series of gathering spaces outdoors, at the same time respecting the garden's formal beginnings. Over the next several years, Pattie and Mason became a gardening team, their complementary skills turning the languishing property into a gorgeous and elegant enclave.

Pattie smiled and said their perfectly refined garden is very much an artistic reflection of Mason's work as a plastic surgeon—in which he adheres to the philosophy that you should change something only enough to bring out its best features and angles. "In surgery, as in gardening, Mason is a perfectionist as well as someone with a vision," Pattie emphasized. I could see how these qualities have come into play over and over in the Williamses' garden.

As much as Pattie credits her husband's talents, her role is hardly secondary. She possesses an expansive knowledge of horticulture and is a discerning researcher who gets things done. There's a hedge of Nellie Stevens holly bordering the driveway, a circle of low American boxwood planted around a dramatic Gillette-designed pool and foun-

TOP: Flowers in containers add brightness and warmth to the gathering and seating spaces, especially when they are separated from the lawn and flowerbeds.

ABOVE: There are extra tablecloths to match for times when additional round tables are set up on the terrace for a large dinner or party.

ABOVE: When they renovated the house, Pattie and Mason wanted a large eat-in kitchen—a friendly place where their two sons and daughter could relax after school. Expanding a tiny brick terrace off the former kitchen ("a utilitarian, servants-only kind of kitchen") into a place for family and friends figured into the greater plan. More bright pink geraniums in pots add color to a full but bloomless bed around a classical sculpture of a blithe figure, dividing this dining area from the rest of the terrace.

LEFT: The clean yet elegant lines of the black ironwork tables and chairs make them perfect choices as terrace furniture. Pattie, a self-styled textiles maven, has unified the several gathering areas on the spacious terrace by mixing and matching cheerfully carefree fabrics on the pillows and cushions. "That way," she emphasizes, "you can toss things any which way and they look right." She makes pillows and cushions in fabrics that go with the variety of flowers in the garden and uses the red-and-white fabrics "for punch."

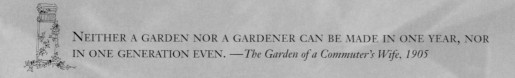

Books on architecture and design line the shelves of the Williamses' library. When it came time to design a classical pergola for the terrace, historical drawings lent ideas and inspiration.

tain, and low beds of azaleas and hydrangeas planted as garden-room dividers.

They began with the terrace—bordered in stone and paved with bricks the same color as the house. But when the construction was completed, in the dog days of summer, their wonderful new terrace "felt like a barge going down the Nile." It was Mason who came up with the idea of a pergola. "The children and I were spending some time in Maine when Mason thought of adding a sheltering pergola off the sunroom," Pattie told me. Working out design details by fax and phone for a classical pergola to harmonize with the garden, Mason had the structure completed by the time Pattie arrived home.

A contented tangle of wisteria—a southern favorite that perfectly suits the garden and the people there—has made itself at home on the pergola, providing deep shade and tight shelter. I'm told there's still work to be done. But, for the time being, the big picture and the hard work are completed. I'm convinced that the Williamses' ultimate reward has to be the spectacular view of green and the knowledge that someone else has to mow the grass.

RIGHT: Hardy geraniums thrive on the sunny terrace.

FOLLOWING PAGES: If "borrowed space" is a term given to the gift of serendipitous vistas of other people's property, then the Williamses received the prize of a panoramic view of country-club greens and fairways. Mason can roll a golf cart through a familiar break in the hydrangeas and head for the nearest hole before dusk for some practice shots. The three young children who used to get drafted into mulching, trimming, and edging duty are grown now, and Pattie admits to having visions of hosting their weddings in her garden

Garden Shelter with a Past
A Grape Arbor Centers a Lawn

THE WEATHERED SURFACE of meandering stone walls, so typical of this picturesque corner of northwestern Connecticut, gives Ted and Sue Ann Marolda's property a sense of authority. These artful structures of local granite appear to have been scattered this way by nature, dividing a spacious lawn and garden around the house into neat and pleasing sections. The walls sculpt garden beds and garden rooms; they create intimacy. But what makes these

PRECEDING PAGE: Leafy vines make the ceiling while stones become the walls in a garden space created inside a grape arbor.

ABOVE: A split-rail gate parts the main stone wall, acting as a kind of portal to the rolling fields and mountains beyond. This stone wall is one of many on the property of Ted and Sue Ann Marolda that Ted built from weathered granite stones. A gate that remains from the property's original picket fencing is seen to the right. The custom-made arch is filling out with silver lace vine, a vine that was started in late spring in the large wooden barrels.

particular dry stone walls even more impressive is their provenance. "I don't play tennis or golf," Ted explained. "I spend my free time building stone walls." Without exception, every stone was scooped from the earth or taken from remnants of collapsing old walls and carried to the property by Ted.

The Sunday I arrived at Haystack Mountain Farm began with an early morning drive north on harrowing Route 95 (the truckers' speedway!), then west to the serene Connecticut village of Norfolk, where I felt as though I had slipped off the highway into a bygone era. Out of habit, I turned off the main road to curl around the village green, where I once rented a lovely old house for a

summer. My hosts for the next several days were good friends who live a mile outside of town on property neighboring the Maroldas'. With a gracious ease no one could feign, Sue Ann welcomed us for dinner that night, the weary traveler and the gardening neighbors. On that evening, she created a picture-perfect table setting and a meal to match. Feeling right at home, I sank into a big wicker chair with a glass of chilled white wine. The five of us ate dinner on a spacious open porch that overlooked Ted's stonework and offered a high view of their grape arbor. The setting sun moved low in the sky, and a magnificent fringe of light turned a canopy of grape leaves into lace.

ABOVE: Originally, the porch area off the kitchen was "uneventful," its steps leading to a patch of lawn. So Ted leveled off the area, paved it with large stones, then added his signature stone wall, using "nice old cut stones that fit perfectly" and a low iron gate. There's just enough room to move a small table and a pair of chairs into the space for a pleasant meal for two.

When Ted and Sue Ann bought Haystack Mountain Farm in 1981, they were enamored of its expansive view of state parkland and its wonderful 1782 farmhouse. Then they discovered a thicket of ancient grapevines—wild Concord grapes, which are native to New England. The vines trailed on the ground in the overgrown backyard near a small porch,

simply described by the couple as "awful." The vines were the hardy survivors of a long-neglected arbor. Entwined with wild honeysuckle, their bases were still thick and healthy. Ted peeled each vine from its honeysuckle vise and spread it on the ground. Then he began to construct the first of several trellises to support the bounty of vines.

The first trellis—a structure made by bracing evenly spaced stripped cedar poles—measured ten feet wide. When Ted tossed the vines on top, they made an instant shelter. After a year, the trellis was doubled in width to accommodate visiting family and friends who always migrated to that part of the yard. The year after that, the trellis was enlarged to a full forty feet, filling much of the lawn that separated it from the formerly "awful" porch, which has undergone its share of renovation and expansion.

The final trellis structure took four years to get right. It features a walkway through the middle, bluestone flooring ("For the color and because it's kinder on high heels," explains Sue Ann), and areas for dining and relaxing at each end. "It's bugless and cool even on the hottest summer nights—and like a wind tunnel when the southwest breeze blows through."

LEFT: Old but healthy Concord grapevines lay in a tangle on the ground, entwined with honeysuckle, until a proper arbor was built for them by the new garden owners. The arbor's five-year-long evolution included expanding the structure in both directions, adding a bluestone floor, and, finally, building dry stone walls to better define the area. In the fall, the grapes are harvested for grape jelly.

ABOVE: Sue Ann has decorated the so-called hidden garden off the kitchen with rose standards, pots of blooming annuals, and distinctive perennials, such as hostas and ferns, as well as kitchen herbs that the deer don't touch because they are so close to the house. The iron finials, used as decorative objects, are new, but have weathered well and look much older.

RIGHT: At one time, the family kept ducks on a nearby pond, so a friend brought the pottery variety—an antique—as a suitable housewarming gift. The big duck does a fine job of holding down the tablecloth. The chairs are, according to Ted and Sue Ann, "the cheap ones, but the grape-leaf motif fits right in." The planted urns—two at each walkway entrance— add color and a pleasing classical shape.

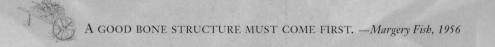

A GOOD BONE STRUCTURE MUST COME FIRST. —*Margery Fish, 1956*

CARRYING TURF, CONNEMARA.

These postcards served as partial inspiration for the weathered "farm" look of Ted Marolda's
stonework at Haystack Mountain Farm. Ted began to work with masonry during his college days,
when he had a summer construction job. He claims that his dry stonework has been influenced
largely by the ubiquitous stone walls of Ireland—the building of which is "a simple process," according
to Ted. But surely it takes more than the luck of the Irish to pull off such an artful arrangement,
which shows a felicitous balance of size and shape and a sharp sense of texture and color.

No visitor could miss Sue Ann's luxuriant flowers ("They're on hormones," she told me confidentially) planted in stylish containers—urns of impatiens announcing both entrances to the arbor, gracefully cascading ferns decorating a charming side porch, elegant rose standards and bright daisies in containers on the porch, and terra-cotta pots placed everywhere.

Even as the arbor project created a significant garden room and focal point, it continued to need something more substantial than bluestone flooring to separate it from the broad expanse of lawn. Stone walls had defined the rest of the property quite well. The success of one wall in particular, which curves gently at the crest of the hill and provides an effective visual break between the garden and the vast mountains beyond, prompted the couple to decide that Ted should abandon any plans for a new hobby until he'd bordered the arbor with another of his stone walls.

Both Ted and Sue Ann grew up in the nearby village of Norfolk, so winnowing down any guest list is an awesome task for them. But entertaining in the grape arbor—now a fully outlined garden room—is always a delightful event.

There's a satisfying division of labor and humor here, as well as an unspoken harmony on matters concerning the home and garden. And strong stone walls linking it all together.

RIGHT: Ted's stonework is brightened by wild roses and bold strokes of peonies (see following pages).

DIVIDED BY THREE
Neighborly Hillside Gardens

MY DESTINATION IS the first of three gardens linked by small-town friendships and common property lines. It's at the end of a narrow street—still just a line on my garishly illustrated tourist's guide to this charming Ozarks town. The map is borrowed and has begun to shred at the creases and near the street in question. If I miss the property, which has no identifying street numbers, I've been told that I'll loop around and wind up right back where I started.

All three gardening neighbors have chosen this quiet street because it's much like living in a secret enclave, even though it lies right in the heart of the bustling and somewhat funky tourist town of Eureka Springs, Arkansas. ("Even people who live on this street think it's a dead end," one tells me confidentially.) But what they treasure most is the lay of the land.

There is hardly a flat, straight surface in all of Eureka Springs—a Victorian-era spa and resort carved into the side of a mountain. Vibrant green foliage tells the tale of a wonderfully rainy spring. At a snail's pace, I wind along what seems like a shady lane, looking forward to seeing how a number of distinctly different personalities have dealt with challenges better suited to billy goats in the Swiss Alps. I've been alerted to look for a pergola on the grounds of the first property, visible from the street even when the old oak trees are heavy with branches. I spot the romantic pergola just before the deceptive curve in the road. I decide I've arrived.

The First Garden
A Spiritual Place

Since 1971, Molly and John Seeligson have lived in a rambling Victorian house with a wide veranda that overlooks their garden, which, by Molly's own admission, is happily overplanted. Called Fair Oaks for a very good reason, it has a big side yard where perennial beds are separated by patches of lawn and bordered boldly with local rocks. Believing that being in your garden brings balance to the rest of your life, the couple wanted a view of the garden from the veranda, as well as a romantic location for Molly's wedding-party business. From the start, the Seeligsons' desire to create a spiritual mood in the garden guided their plan.

When the Seeligsons acquired the property, the garden at Fair Oaks had been allowed to grow wild and reckless for forty years. Despite a steepness that could turn a rolling wheelbarrow into a guided missile, the couple says they liked the natural contours of

their hilly new yard and wanted to work with it rather than change it. I paused to admire delicate blue irises in one of the higher beds, but gravity compelled me to explore the lower plantings and a vegetable garden that stops abruptly at a line of tall trees and a steep ravine just beyond.

Molly, the main gardener in the family, tried to explain how far they'd come. "There was a thick overgrowth of brambles—non-producing wild berry vines, very sticky to remove—and exactly three peonies. We'd sit out on our nice porch over dinner and try so hard to visualize a garden in that wildness." Then Molly described how the clearing operation began.

The Seeligsons and various able-bodied volunteers began to loosen and pull up the overgrowth by the roots, starting at the top, near the street. A team of mules seems almost quaint, but these surefooted beasts of

ABOVE: Sited at the crest of a significant slope, the classically designed pergola overlooks a series of circular perennial beds, ringed by borders of prominent local stones. White wicker chairs, easily replaced with a dining arrangement in the same spot, add to the romantic Victorian garden room with a view.

LEFT: "We wanted children in the garden always," Molly told me. The fountain, surrounded by mature hydrangeas just coming into bloom, carries out the charming Victorian motif.

burden were well suited to uprooting the honeysuckle vines mixed with berry brambles and the indescribable weeds and denser vegetation. "We rolled all the plant material into one mass," then let the weight of the uprooted earth roll down the hill—"a kind of gigantic jelly roll." The Seeligsons built up confined flower beds on the hillside of their clean canvas, mostly perennials and things that grow well in that part of the country. They put in conspicuous numbers of the cheerful coneflowers that thrive along the highways of Arkansas. They also planted azaleas for a splash of color in the spring.

When their son outgrew his sandbox, located a strategic distance from the house and in the shade of a wonderful oak tree, that spot became the perfect place for outdoor seating and gathering. A classic pergola design seemed in keeping with the romantic feeling of the Victorian house and the heady profusion of old-fashioned flowers. It would face southeast and benefit from good light all day. When a designer friend from France visited the family for six weeks, he constructed the pergola's four massive columns using chicken-wire skeletons to support wet cement. A towering and impressive focal point, this was clearly not a project for the fainthearted.

The entire garden has a serenity about it, but the lavishly planted area around the pergola is idyllic and, according to Molly, "a serene place to reconnect with your spirit."

L E F T : Leafy wisteria and large-leaved begonias on a cover of pink impatiens surround a classical stone bench.

THIS BUD OF LOVE BY SUMMER'S RIPENING BREATH
MAY PROVE A BEAUTEOUS FLOWER WHEN NEXT WE MEET. —*William Shakespeare, c.1596*

Throughout the year, brides and bridegrooms with small wedding parties—ten or fewer people,
"so as not to disturb the tone of the neighborhood"—take their vows under the Seeligsons' pergola, then pose
on a circular stone bench for an official portrait, taken by Molly Seeligson. Molly's own vow is to
finally organize the many boxes of keepsake photos for an album.

PHOTOGRAPHS: MOLLY SEELIGSON

THE SECOND GARDEN
AN ENTERTAINING PLACE

It's a short but arduous downhill walk from the Seeligson garden to the Douglass garden. The Douglasses' steep property is stopped at its farthest point by a high stone wall that drops twelve feet to a narrow and winding street below, where passing is a gamble and parking is next to impossible. Their rambling Victorian house appears to be perched there for its panoramic view of the town. A long stone stairway connects the upper garden to the house and ends at a nearby stone-walled terrace.

Irene and Bill Douglass have a low-maintenance, high-pleasure attitude about the hilly garden they "inherited" nearly a decade ago. They are quick to admit that they can't take much credit for the well-terraced property, where platforms and levels provide places to sit and enjoy life amid a sea of green foliage and shrubbery. The former owners had chipped away at the stubborn hillside, creating cozy spaces for gathering. The present owners had the good taste to recognize that this effort made the place perfectly suited for their outdoor lifestyle. The terrace offers a rare level area in this garden,

LEFT: Two vintage-looking metal porch chairs, comfortably homey, are tucked into a corner on one level of a long stairway that leads from the higher of two entrances. The tabletop, which rests on an old iron base from a junk shop, was picked up at a local quarry several years ago for the bargain price of twenty-five dollars.

TOO LATE I STAYED—FORGIVE THE CRIME!/UNHEEDED FLEW THE HOURS;/HOW NOISELESS FALLS THE FOOT OF TIME/THAT ONLY TREADS ON FLOWERS. —*William Robert Spencer (1770-1834)*

GOING-A-MAYING.

Oh! ring the bells, Oh! ring the bells!
  We bid you all, "Good morning;"
Give thanks we pray, our flowers are gay,
  And fair for your adorning.

Oh! ring the bells, Oh! ring the bells!
  Good friends, accept our greeting;
Where we have been, the woods are green,
  And fast the Spring is fleeting.

Oh! ring the bells, Oh! ring the bells!
  For this fair time of Maying;
We blossoms bring, and while we sing,
  Oh! hark to what we're saying.

44

AT THE GATE.

"PAPA and Mamma have gone to the town,
  And they said, if a very good girl, I would be;
That they would be home, when the Sun went down,
  And bring back some pretty new toys for me.

And dear Mamma said, with a kiss and a smile,
  "I'll look for a dolly, a dolly so gay;
With pretty pink slippers, and long yellow curls,
  To come here and play with my baby some day."

I've tried to be good, and my lessons I know,
  And out at the gate, I am waiting to see—
Oh! there they are now, at the foot of the hill,
  And soon I shall know, what they're bringing to me!"

"We're always on the lookout for artwork from old children's books to frame," the Douglasses say. These loose pages from a book of children's poetry illustrated by Kate Greenaway are from their collection. "The garden scenes have become our favorites."

where food and drinks, not to mention colorful potted plants, can be set on the wall. It's a spot tailor-made for entertaining.

"We are in town, but secluded," Bill told me as I attempted to steady my tripod on a jagged outcropping of rocks for a shot of metal porch chairs painted a sassy shade of green. "When people, especially tourists, walk by our house, they see only a huge Victorian stone wall. We have a fabulous view and plenty of privacy."

The composition of the garden beds is dictated by the presence of the many levels, walls, and walkways. "We plant cheerful annuals and perennials when the garden needs dressing up and a shot of color," Irene said. "Once a year, we rake and fertilize. Our sloping garden is wonderfully maintenance-free." Otherwise, the Douglasses are happy with soft ground covers underfoot and the natural wildness, with its lush native vegetation that creeps into rocky slopes.

The couple prefers intimate gatherings. They have a stone table that seats eight comfortably. For larger affairs, there is no lack of seating on steps and ledges, where guests balance plates on laps. In contrast to the decorating style of their traditional home, the garden sculpture and accessories are contemporary—stone and stainless steel. "We like to

use the garden rooms to express our taste for the modern," Bill said. Appropriately, all the tables are stone—limestone from the local quarry—and need only to be waterproofed on a yearly basis. Iron chairs are low-maintenance as well; when the weather is nice for long periods, the cushions stay out, in anticipation of visitors who are good at following directions. At night, the lights of Eureka Springs twinkle across the valley. A string of "our tacky little Christmas lights" on the porch year-round twinkles back.

ABOVE: Irene and Bill Douglass's terrace is situated at the property's lowest point, near an old retaining wall made of stone. This also happens to be one of the highest vistas overlooking the old Victorian town of Eureka Springs, Arkansas. The house may be authentically Victorian, but the garden furnishings are contemporary and eclectic (see also page 169). A substantial dining table, made of a massive slab of local limestone, is rarely moved from its place, for obvious reasons. The scale of the large stone pagoda harmonizes with the sizeable table. At nightfall, a candle inside the pagoda can be lighted. The lion "came with the house."

AN ORIENTAL TOUCH

Since our schedules on the day of my visit were in conflict, Gary Eagan and Steve Beacham suggested that I take a solitary self-guided tour of their garden. Enthusiastically, they filled me in by phone on what to expect, which at first sounded as though they had recreated China in the Ozarks. Yet I trusted their taste, possibly because I had recently discovered these artisans' fine handcrafted pottery in a local shop. Gary's work is inspired by the Arts and Crafts movement; Steve's is more whimsical and delicately intricate. All this prompted me to wonder just what I would find in their garden and filled me with new energy for the climb.

A high fence separates the garden and the Victorian house from the rest of the world. Massive and primitive double wooden doors stand in place of a conventional front gate. They squeak in low tones, as if to announce the arrival of guests. The lot is more confined than its neighbors, yet the hilly property has been planned with skill around a theme. As soon as I closed the doors behind me, I was transported to an exotic place.

RIGHT: In China, if a garden is small, it's divided into even smaller "rooms" to make it seem larger. This theory was put to effective use on the modest hilly property that surrounds Gary Eagan and Steve Beacham's Victorian house. A wooden bridge connects two ponds, creating a water feature; the table and chairs establish a gathering area; the open arched doorway leads to a tiny room beyond. Tall slatted wood fencing holds it all together.

ABOVE: Wooden-plank fencing plays an important part in this garden's design. It provides privacy in a neighborhood of closely built homes, a backdrop that enhances the garden's various plantings, and a wall on which to hang artwork. Stone plaques, bearing botanical designs in relief, decorate the fence as though they were pictures on the walls of an interior living room.

Gary and Steve's overall vision for the hilly slopes of Eureka Springs is for a natural space that evokes the streams and forests of the Ozarks and at the same time is overlaid by the Oriental philosophy of garden design—the Southeast meets the Far East. They know the terrain well, having gardened in this part of the country since the mid-1960s, and having tended this special garden since 1979.

"Gary and I have taken a rather barren space and transformed it," Steve acknowl-edged. Right away, I saw that their garden is dominated by the shade from its large oak trees. In 1979, the garden had much more direct sunlight than it does now, mainly because the secondary layer of trees—Japanese maples and dogwood—have grown considerably since then and have changed the ecosystem. A beautiful iris collection has given way to hostas; sunny bloomers have been replaced by shade-loving plants.

The garden started out as a rocky patch of yard. It had a straggly privet hedge, overgrown mock orange bushes, and very little else. Gary and Steve divided the space in a logical and functional way, paying attention to the footpaths they instinctively made during their daily strolls. As a result, a formal stone path starts at the gate and meanders through the garden. The potters used shards from their own broken pieces in the cement joins of the path, along with small stones. The overgrown bushes and hedge were removed, then a fence was added to provide privacy and define the space. After three Japanese trees had been planted along the wooden fence line, a stone patio was next on the construction plan.

After a vacation in China in the 1980s, a serendipitous Oriental influence began to alter the couple's style and their greater garden plan. When we met the day after my first visit for (iced American) tea on the patio, Gary explained that, in China, if a garden is too small, it's divided into even smaller spaces to make it seem larger. Near the patio, there's an arched doorway that leads to a pocket-sized garden room and frames a leafy

ABOVE: The garden's ornate aluminum furniture was painted black to resemble iron. The patio is the only area of this small garden that allows for group seating, so planning it correctly was essential to the rest of the plan.

RIGHT: A serene Eastern mood is immediately set by the garden's big double doors, which open from the street onto the property. Occasional touches, such as the decorative pagoda and the incidental rocks standing on end (called *tai hu* in Chinese), carry out the theme without overwhelming it.

view of bamboo. In that space, there are unusually shaped rocks standing on end or placed on pedestals just off the ground. I'm told that in China, these are called *tai hu*. "Some of the rocks weigh 250 pounds, so we devised a sling to carry them to chosen spots," Gary explained. It amuses me that even the garden's construction techniques reveal influences of the Orient.

The patio, built on a terraced plane and handsomely furnished with painted aluminum pieces that look just like iron, is shaded by white and pink pruned dogwood trees, which create a wide summertime umbrella. The cozy seating area looks down upon the garden's two fish ponds. Pumps feed the pools of water and also create a series of pleasant meandering streams on the property. A small wooden arched bridge links the pools. By making use of Oriental design concepts, this bridge gives the illusion that the two pools are in fact one large pond.

At night, a well-designed electrical system paints light on rocks, trees, and other focal areas. Other lights illuminate the paths. Gary and Steve point out that the great pleasure of their patio area is being able to sit and enjoy views of the other garden rooms, day or night. In China, this concept of ultimate peace can be expressed as *wu shang an ning*. This phrase seems quite at home in this transformed garden in the Ozarks.

LEFT: Steve and Gary's peonies thrive in their tranquil environment.

THERE IS A KIND OF IMMORTALITY IN EVERY GARDEN. —*Gladys Taber, 1955*

*A vacation to China taken during the 1980s, documented with
countless snapshots, completely changed the mood and the plan of Gary Eagan
and Steve Beacham's garden-in-progress.*

STROLLING THE SKYLINE
A Terrace Turned Pocket Park

IT WAS A scorcher—yet another record-setting July afternoon in New York City. But I was content as I cooled off over iced tea in Anne Newman and Joe Bacal's garden. The shade of a stout Norway spruce provided blessed relief from the setting sun, which insisted on dazzling us by reflecting hotly off the shimmering Hudson River. With thoughts of breezier days, Anne told me about a pair of doves that laid two eggs nearby last spring; peregrine

falcons, which majestically swoop overhead; as well as other garden regulars including hawks and jays, not to mention a steady stream of migratory birds on their customary paths. With a sense of awe, we paused to watch a dragonfly alight on a spiky branch. This might not have seemed so remarkable a show of nature were I not eighteen floors above the streets of Manhattan, a city where a plot of earth even the size of a postage stamp is a rarity.

The garden is a spacious and charming rooftop terrace. When the couple were married in 1987, Anne—a southern California native—put an open-air garden space at the top of her list of requirements for a city apartment, something I understand completely. Even though I've spent my entire adult life in New York City, I consider myself a country girl from Maryland still. Yet, by happenstance, I've never lived higher than the seventh floor. My only experience with city gardening was a tiny terrace, which had more audacious pigeons and traffic fumes than possibilities for blooming things.

Anne dismissed my envious comments by telling me it's not as glamorous as it seems. In the beginning, their L-shaped terrace had only a granny-apple tree placed where the walkway makes the turn, one lonely window box of sad-looking verbena, and a root-bound maple tree defying the odds for city survival. More significantly, they found themselves confronting a migraine's worth of structural problems before any long-term garden plans could be made.

"When you live up here, you're responsi-

ble for what happens to the people who live below you. Every leak from a potted plant becomes your immediate concern," Joe explained. So every square foot of the leaky tile flooring was replaced with large terra-cotta-colored pavers, which, in an emergency, can be pulled up. Eager to do some roll-up-your-sleeves gardening, the couple brought in a variety of large planters and containers and transformed the terrace into a thriving place with a California spirit. Unfortunately, watering by hand soon became a way of life.

"A planted terrace is all about watering," Anne said as she described their solution.

They located a terrace designer, Halstead Wells, who's a member of a unique breed: a city gardening engineer, or a so-called urban forester. Relying on Halstead's expertise, the couple installed an effective and straightforward watering system that reaches to every

container through an automated zoning system. The placement of the watering system's copper piping, which runs along the base of the exterior walls, as well as the many flexible plastic "straws," which feed the different flowers and plantings, was determined largely by where Anne and Joe planned to create outdoor rooms for sitting, reading, napping, entertaining alfresco, and, of course, for gazing at the ever-changing view.

The couple also bought a party-size barbecue grill (city ordinances allow the charcoal models) and placed it in an ample yet private alcove perfect for entertaining. But even this sheltered place had its obstacles. When a powerful gust of wind lifted the top off the dining table and smashed it, the first priority in buying any new garden furniture became its weight.

Creating a rustic trellis of birch and cedar, secured with willow lashing, to humanize the

LEFT: When the climbing hydrangea has completed its blooming cycle on the Adirondack-style trellis, Anne adds color and drama to the greenery for special occasions with cut impostors bought at a flower market nearby. The stems are slipped into individual plastic florist's vials, filled with fresh water, and sealed tightly.

FACING, TOP: From the start, Anne Newman and Joe Bacal knew they wanted a walk on their L-shaped rooftop terrace to feel like a stroll through Central Park. They've accomplished this by planting carefully selected shrubbery, small trees, perennials, and annuals in myriad containers and by keeping the plantings happy with a watering system—a must for any large terrace garden. A cafe table and chairs have been set in a strategic spot on the walkway.

FACING, BOTTOM: The hammock belongs to Joe's son Matthew, whose bedroom windows overlook this far end of the terrace, where he has the space all to himself.

high brick walls should have been simple; however, the 1928 building prohibits anything from being attached permanently to the exterior structure. Again, Halstead worked with Anne and Joe to design removeable trellises that hang from a series of extended iron hooks, which loop over the tops of the terrace walls and in turn hang from the edge of the roof. The other ends are bolted to the backs of the terrace's many large containers and planters, lush with hydrangea and honeysuckle.

From the start, Anne and Joe knew they wanted a stroll on their terrace to feel like a walk in the park. They planted privet in an old whiskey barrel across from the granny-apple tree, which shares its space with butterfly-bush. Large wooden planters were made in sections in case they had to be moved. The planters, which are set along the walkway, hold three varieties of clematis, to provide colorful blooms throughout the growing season; taxus pine, often sculpted into interesting shapes by the wind; and ornamental dogwood. Quick-spreading

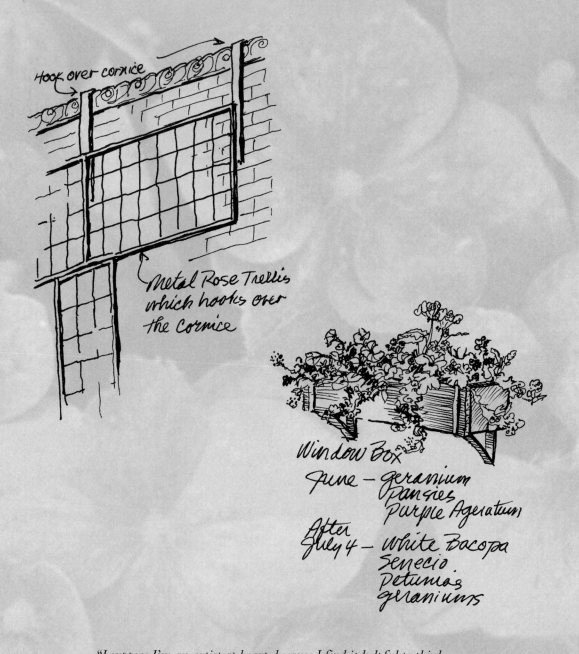

Hook over cornice

Metal Rose Trellis
which hooks over
the cornice

Window Box
June — Geranium
Pansies
Purple Ageratum
After
July 4 — White Bacopa
Senecio
Petunias
Geraniums

"I suppose I'm an artist at heart, because I find it helpful to think
on paper," said Anne Newman about the visual notes she makes for her
window-box plantings as well as other garden ventures.

alyssum—white and purple—makes a delicate ground cover at the base of the ornamental crab-apple trees.

Because of size problems, window boxes had to be custom made. "We start with *Ageratum* and pansies, and later in the summer, we add *Senecio* and white trailing *Bacopa*," Anne told me, her fondness for a pastel palette—delicately hued cosmos, pink geraniums, deep purple petunias—showing at that midsummer moment. Perhaps because both Joe and Anne are in the entertainment business, they definitely know how to light a scene. As the sun sets, up comes the terrace's subtle and effective lighting system: high floodlights mounted at regular intervals under the roofline; a line of five whimsical bell-shaped lights beaming on a straight line of flower boxes; and individual spotlights illuminating the trees.

There's yet another advantage to living so far above the fray. Enjoying a metropolitan voyeur's view of the cityscape, I noticed a lively cocktail party in progress on a terrace across the wide avenue that runs in front of the building. Then I glimpsed a grand Mediterranean-style terrace a block south. With its salmon-colored stucco walls, tall French doors softly curved at the crown, and diaphanous curtains billowing in the breeze, it evoked Hollywood's romantic past.

At that very moment, a glint of metal from the river came into view: as it sailed closer, we could discern the shapes of a long barge and a mighty tug. Then the muffled drone of traffic, punctuated by the shriek of a siren, drifted over the scalloped parapet, bringing everyone back to reality.

Many Rooms of Her Own
Creating Whimsical Spaces and Solitary Places

Growing up in New Jersey, also known as the Garden State, may have had an influence on the career of avid gardener Pat Laltrella. Indeed, gardening has been a recurring theme throughout her life and work, beginning with fond child-hood memories of her relatives' faithfully tended gardens.

There was an aunt who grew a remarkable tree from a peach pit ("I was never able to duplicate this feat," Pat admits); a grandfather who brought a fig tree from Italy and

cultivated rows of grapevines for his own wine-making ("As a child, the possibilities were amazing to me," Pat says); and another aunt who taught Pat how to compost table scraps and the many fish heads that were tossed in a heap after her uncle's frequent fishing expeditions. "My first garden was a vegetable garden, and the seed catalogs just kept coming!" she jokes. Today, a love for her subject is quickly apparent in the flowers she paints and in her garden, which is as artfully composed as a well-planned canvas.

Pat Laltrella's two-story farmhouse, circa 1800, sits on half an acre of land that has the feeling of a spacious old-fashioned farm. There's a cornfield where the property ends in the back and a long meadow across a narrow dirt road in the front. Though the neighbors are only seconds away, they're hidden by the property's original trees.

When Pat bought the house, she inherited the property's full hydrangeas, currant bushes, pear trees, and wild rosebushes. Taking

PRECEDING PAGES: Lavender-painted cedar posts hold a distinctive solid steel gate that has been painted black. It leads to the "secret garden." Pat collaborated with Pennsylvania welder Jack Edmonds, who embellished the original idea with a diamond motif and graceful Gothic lines. Blue stepping stones cover cedar mulch in this year-old area until the creeping lemon thyme can spread into a soft carpet. The mood here is peaceful, with fragrant lavender for relaxation. There are plants to touch and crush between your fingers—scented geraniums, pineapple mint, and chocolate mint—in addition to the lemon thyme.

ABOVE: Influenced by memories of a visit to Sicily, the gardener chose blue slate for the flooring and a dolphin-motif birdbath made by a local Italian craftsman for the "Italian garden." The wooden folding chair was found at a garage sale.

FACING: The yellow flowers of heliopsis separate the Spanish garden from a secluded spot where the weathered bench offers a break for the weary gardener. The old metal piece was found in a small barn on the property and seems to have been part of a horse-drawn machine that dug furrows. Now it stands vertically as a piece of garden sculpture.

care to leave the natural treasures in place, Pat resisted the temptation to "fill the many unplanted spaces to see results." Instead, she created separate beds one by one, giving rise quite spontaneously to fanciful "rooms" with distinctive personalities, which no plan could have anticipated.

"One day, I viewed the property from a second-floor window and—just like that—decided I would replace every blade of grass with color," Pat told me as we stood by a handcrafted gate leading to the perennial garden, the first and still the primary garden. "I began to see the flat expanse as a level foundation for rooms, similar to the rooms of my simple farmhouse, which I've decorated to bring back memories of travel to other cultures. I'll set my stereo speakers

PRECEDING PAGES: The old chair used to have a place in Pat's kitchen, then found its way out of doors. When she neglected to bring the chair inside, "It became a sculptural piece the next spring." This seat is best appreciated for its form rather than for its function.

ABOVE: In the Spanish garden, a rusted tin lantern—actually a decoratively cut tin can—holds a votive candle and sits on a weathered bench next to a collection of cactus.

ABOVE RIGHT: A clay chandelier, found in Mexico, provides additional lighting.

in the windows and find inspiration in a lively tango or in the intense melody of a Spanish guitar."

Inside the house, the kitchen is Italian in style, and it's hard to miss a wall of brightly decorated ceramic plates. The bathroom is Florida all the way—Miami Beach pinks and turquoises. The dining room goes upscale with English pieces, while the sitting room has a distinctive Spanish accent. Set off from the rest of the house, the living room glows with the same soft yellows and pinks found outside in the perennial garden. As I toured

the inside of Pat Laltrella's house, I realized that her interior rooms have corresponding themes in the numerous small garden rooms outdoors. "The outside is just an extension of the inside—another place to put my collections," she explains.

Rather than build raised beds to delineate spaces—a valid plan for flat expanses—this gardener settled on gaining needed height from her choice of trees and shrubs within each room. Ever since she was a child, Pat's loved the gentle crunching sound of small pebbles when they're walked upon, so it was only a matter of time before every pathway was made up of natural elements, such as stones and crushed slate, to break up the straight lines of the land.

As the "rooms" expanded, they seemed to wander off visually into the cornfield beyond. To control the view as well as to mark the property's end, Pat installed a four-foot-high open-slatted wooden fence. With this remarkable improvement, the individual gardens "returned" to their areas. In fact, they became stronger focal points, making

WE KNOW NOTHING THAT WILL CULTIVATE A TASTE FOR THE FASCINATING ART OF GARDENESQUE DESIGNING, AND PRODUCE A QUICK RETURN OF PLEASURE FOR THE TIME SPENT, AS THE STUDY OF PAPER PLANS FOR ONE'S OWN GROUNDS. IGNORANT GARDENERS, AND SELF-SUFFICIENT BUSINESS MEN WHO KNOW NOTHING ABOUT GARDENING, ARE APT TO INDULGE IN RIDICULE OF THIS PAPER GARDENING, BUT IT IS THE RIDICULE ONLY WHICH IS RIDICULOUS. —*Frank J. Scott, 1881*

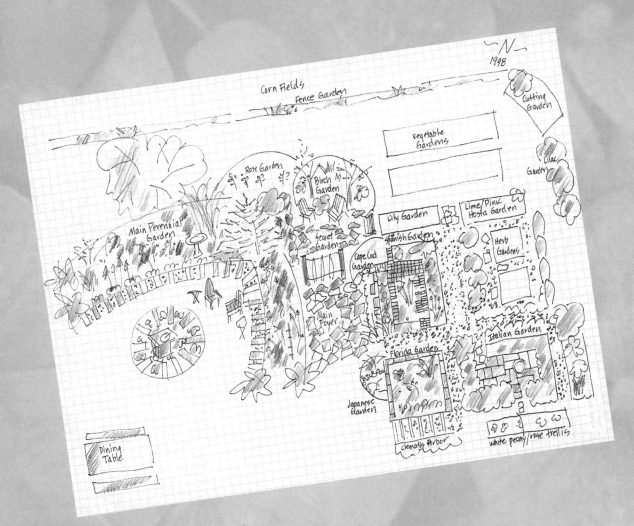

Pat Laltrella swears that you don't have to be an artist (which she is) to devise a plan in color for your garden spaces. She likes the accurate scale that graph paper ensures and advises careful measurement and plotting the overall garden layout in pencil. A color plan helps you see how plantings contrast. The position of shade trees will, to some extent, determine the comfort of guests on a hot day. But beyond these rough guidelines, she suggests exploring the possibilities for plants and for people in the garden.

ABOVE: The flooring of Pat Laltrella's garden is as varied as the patterns and styles inside the home of a collector of fine carpets. You turn a corner and the flooring changes from soft mulch to crunchy pebbles; around the bend, you find creeping thyme padding a floor of slate. The variety is astounding, especially in this modest space.

the half-acre plot appear larger. Still, Pat could enjoy the texture of the cornfield between the slats, which, in a serendipitous way, gave rise to the linear "fence garden," trimmed by the clear blues and soft yellows found in the iris, coreopsis, Harrison yellow antique roses, and foxgloves that grow there.

Color has always been a priority for Pat. The design of each room begins with the

selection of favorite plantings, then branches out to include the choice of a complementary color and texture for the "flooring." Next, sculptural and found pieces of furniture add to the mood—they must be tried-and-true old pieces from antiques shops and yard sales with histories to match the house, and they must be sturdy, with an ability to age gracefully. After that, Pat searches her cherished souvenirs to come up with "garden room accessories that make me smile."

The second time I visited, camera and equipment in hand, the rising sun had just begun to cast a soft glow on every part of the garden—the perfect light for capturing on film the nuances of a gardener's creative hand. I revisited each garden room. In the meantime, my host set down a welcome pot of coffee (the pot and the cups looked predictably vintage). Out of the corner of my eye, I saw a plate piled high with English scones, which I was sure were home-baked and hot from the oven. As I waited for the light to shift to a bed of deep green hostas, Pat kept me company. "I need my solitude in this place. Still, it's necessary that friends and neighbors share my pride," she told me.

As I tried to decide on my favorite spot in this country garden with its inviting warren of rooms, I understood just how they feel.

RIGHT: Pat snapped up the large urn at a local antiques shop because it reminded her of the many urns she'd seen on vacations in Sicily. Her favorite urn holds a clay pot filled with creeping sedum that sends its seeds down to the pebble walkway, where they take root.

Key to Additional Flora

4: Zinnias, asters, and others

6/7: Pansies and ornamental cabbage

20: Rose

34: Peonies

46: Agapanthus

48: Rose, agapanthus

58: Apples

60: Hydrangea

74: Euphorbia

84: Magnolia grandiflora

86: Dianthus

98: Pinks

106: Ornamental cabbage

122: Wild shrub roses

130: Rose

132: Dahlia

143: Wisteria

144: Hydrangeas

156: Bearded iris

168: Japanese tree peony

177: Ferns

186: Yarrow

194: Daylily "Evergold"